Shame-Less Lives,

~

Grace-Full Congregations

Shame-Less Lives,

~

Grace-Full Congregations

Karen A. McClintock

The Alban Institute
Herndon, Virginia

The Alban Institute
2121 Cooperative Way, Suite 100
Herndon, VA 20171

Cover design by Signal Hill.

Library of Congress Cataloging-in-Publication Data
McClintock, Karen A., 1953-
Shame-less lives, grace-full congregations / Karen A. McClintock.
p. cm.
Includes bibliographical references.
ISBN 978-1-56699-424-8
1. Shame–Religious aspects–Christianity. 2. Shame. I. Title. II. Title:
Shameless lives, gracefull congregations.
BT714.M35 2011
233'.5–dc23
2011042838

12   13   14   15   16   UG   5   4   3   2   1

Contents

Acknowledgments

For by grace you have been saved through faith, and this is not your own doing; it is the gift of God.

Ephesians 2:8

My first acknowledgment is that I only partially claim this work as my own. I have had many teachers on the journey toward grace, and I tell many of their stories. Because I hold personal information as a sacred trust, however, I have changed names, genders, and situations to illustrate common themes or directly asked permission to use a story. I am grateful to many people who will never know that they have been my teachers.

I thank my liberating counselors Frank, Thora, Bill, and Jim, who have spent more time with my soul than most and have taken great care with it. I thank my parents (who are dancing in heaven these days) for teaching me love, despite the fact that secrets about my father's sexual orientation left us with shame. My sister's quiet support and eagerness to have me tell the story have been very healing for me. I am always in awe and gratitude for my daughter's grace toward me and others in her family. I waited more than thirty years to meet the love of my life, who is now my dear grace-providing husband and know how lucky I am that he embodies the gospel for me every blessed day.

Once a week for the past twenty years, I have met with a group of women to write down our hopes, tragedies, unfulfilled dreams, lost loves, and great erotic moments, either real or imagined. With their permission I name Marcy, Darrelle, Liz, Janet, Alice, and Ann and thank them for gracing my writing journey and refining my prose. My editor of several books, Beth Gaede, has been a great and trusted companion for this journey. She knows how to inspire the best in her writers without shame, which is no small task, and I am thankful that we share a passionate vision for shame-less leaders and faith communities.

Introduction

My parents were graceful dancers. Their courtship and marriage developed along with the sounds of Benny Goodman and Jimmy Dorsey. They perfected the two-step, the fox trot, the jitterbug, and more. They often went to dance clubs and then returned home to dance a little longer around the living room. I come from a line of elegant people.

So I wasn't surprised when my parents made clear to my older sister and me that we would attend the Jeanne Borsky School of Dance. We were expected to learn charm and to achieve perfect grace. My parents believed dance was one of my callings. They said that I walked around the living room on the tips of my toes at the age of two, so we all hoped for my future stardom. As soon as my feet were strong enough to be crammed into little satin toe shoes, my mother took me to enroll in class.

In our pink tights and black leotards, fifteen delicate, bouncy girls lined up along the bar to practice our turnout. In walked Jeanne Borsky. She glided along the floor. Her hair was pinned up high on her head, and she wore thick pancake makeup, as if she were still in the spotlight on stage. She was old, yet ageless. I wanted to be graceful like Mrs. Borsky. She was perfectly balanced, flexible, and strong. This must be grace.

When she said, "Good morning, students," I became her devoted protégé.

This moment quickly faded as we got down to the work of being graceful. The music had a beat that I found I couldn't keep, Mrs. Borsky's smile began to fade, and before long I felt as awkward as a young giraffe taking his first steps. I forced my body into stretches and movements that felt more like contortions than beautiful extensions.

I learned that comparison is a form of shame. In ballet training you have to look exactly like the others. We were all mercilessly compared to the best students in the class. We were shamed for not properly executing the steps, for not conveying the right feelings, for not having the right body shape, for anything short of perfection. We soon learned to do each move correctly or else—the "else" being Mrs. Borsky's black cane, which she used to rap us on the inside of the knee if our turnout wasn't turned out far enough.

Here is what I learned about grace (and shame) at Mrs. Borsky's. I learned that grace can be achieved only through hard work. I learned that grace is not free: either your parents pay for the lessons or you do. I learned that grace doesn't come naturally. I learned that I couldn't become graceful out of my desire to dance; I had to overcome my unworthiness by righteous hard work. Only when I had achieved the perfect line, the perfect form, the perfect leap into the air, then, maybe, I could enjoy the riches of grace.

Forty years later, I am still shaking off the ill effects of the shame I learned at Jeanne Borsky's School of Dance. And maybe you haven't shaken off the cultural and church-taught idea that grace must be earned through hard work and self-incrimination. This attitude has sometimes been called works righteousness. Jokes are made about the infliction of shame by Jewish mothers, Catholic nuns, and a whole host of other religious teachers. But no matter what the origin of the "shoulds" and the "oughts," we too often live more in shame than in grace.

After years of studying shame and overcoming no small amount of my own, I have come to see shame and grace differently. I also see my old ballet teacher differently. Jeanne Borsky knew a lot about ballet and a lot about shame, but she didn't really know a thing about grace. Even though her body was flexible, strong, and well shaped, as a teacher, she was mean spirited and her behaviors were ugly. I still vividly remember the humiliation of being made to repeatedly leap in front of the others, only to have her make another disparaging comment. I remember looking in the mirror and thinking of myself as misshapen and inadequate. This was not the experience I had hoped for or the one my parents had wanted for me.

Jeanne was a shame-driven leader. I now wonder what experiences led her to such a place of negativity. I wonder if her dreams of stardom had fallen apart at some point in her career. I wonder if she had made her dancing the focus of her life to such an extent that her relationships had gone awry. Perhaps having given so much attention to beauty and physical prowess, she had grown more shame-laden as she watched her own body age. After years of trying to be physically perfect, she never experienced her own grace and beauty in such a way that she could pass those lessons along to us. Without greater self-worth, she didn't know how to build our self-esteem along with strong and competent physiques. She couldn't make genuine grace happen. What a shame that was!

How Does Shame Take Hold?

I can only speculate on the causes of my dance teacher's pain, but I know she is not unique in carrying and passing along shame. Shame begins in childhood and sneaks up on us during adolescence, and we hear it in the voices of our parents and peers. Sometimes we internalize those voices, and they become our own self-shaming messengers. In this book you will learn that what you say to yourself about yourself matters. This book will help you to identify the source or sources of your shame and heal them. Once you've done that, you can move beyond cycles of shame that feed strongly into addictive behaviors, codependency, noxious secrets, and problematic relationships. This book will also guide you in liberating others from their shame, be they friends, colleagues, or people in a congregation where you worship and serve.

One contribution to my dance teacher's shame and to all of our experiences of shame is that we live in a "we try harder" culture. Driven by a society of consumption, we are told by the media that what we have is not enough. And because we are valued by what we have or do not have, we are also told that *who we are* is not enough. Driven by a society that markets products to make us "perfect," we experience our own inadequacy on a daily basis. We aren't smart enough, talented enough, or beautiful enough to attract an equally smart, talented, and beautiful mate or to become the top sales manager in the company or to produce and raise children who will bring home the "Best in Class" bumper sticker for the back of the new car.

If the marketing media can convince us of our unworthiness in any arena, we are more likely to purchase their products. We are told to overcome our failures with more and more effort. Even pleasure is seen only as a reward for hard work and financial status. If you work eighty hours a week and overtime, you can earn enough money for the cruise that you "deserve." An ad says, "You deserve a break today, so go out and get away" for some burgers and fries. Companies both great and small rely on us to overcompensate for our overproductivity with the desire to purchase more products that will help us to have more fun.

Sometimes when I speak with people about increasing the amount of pleasure and play in their lives they say, "I'll try it" or "I know I should *work* on that." We are encouraged by the dominant culture to self-improve rather than self-affirm and to strive for more rather than be content with what is and satisfied with ourselves. The pervasive and soul-defeating presence of cultural shame leads to perfectionism, addiction, and self-hatred. When the workplaces we give our time to and the family back home convince us that we are unworthy, we compensate for that feeling with more hard work, more success, and inevitably more major purchases to ward off that niggling feeling that maybe, just maybe, we are still not good enough. In the end, every life lesson feels more like a whack on the knee than a moment of grace and acceptance. When our lives are weighed down with shame, we find it difficult to be graceful.

It is my intention that this book will take you on a journey in which you uncover, analyze, and heal your own shame. What do you say to yourself that weighs you down? Do you find yourself sounding like your mother or your old boss or your ex-wife? You are fine one minute and the next you say something quite terrible to yourself, and even wonder, "Where did that come from?" You have internalized the critical voices of others and use them to measure your performance in the present day. You may think that this shame is yours alone and that you must carry it in silence or in secret. You may also think that no one else is affected by it. I suspect that you are fooling yourself. Your attitudes, feelings, and sense of self-worth affect everyone in your sphere of influence. And, like my dance teacher, you cannot uplift others without feeling positive about yourself. Your shame affects everyone around you, even if it is unspoken or disowned.

SHAME AT CHURCH

While readers of this book come from many different theological backgrounds, I ask you to explore the shame-laden messages within your own religious teachings and practices. What we learn in Sunday school or Sabbath school and what we hear from preachers and rabbis shape our core self-esteem. Were you taught that you are a child of God, created in God's image? Have you been repeatedly told that you have committed unpardonable sins? How you see yourself may be directly connected to religious teachings about your goodness and your shamefulness.

I began teaching about sexual shame in congregations more than a decade ago. In workshops I frequently comment that everyone in the room is still carrying around shame. One day a clergyman in the back of a huge hall of people stood and declared that he had no shame at all. We were all silent for a moment in disbelief. I said, "What a blessing," but I am still curious about that man. How did he dodge the shame bullet? How did he avoid making this common story *his* story? Clergy and leaders in congregations are often the most shame-bound people I have encountered. People with a good deal of inner pain and a deep sense of unworthiness frequently find their way to faith communities. Many of those enter congregational leadership in an unconscious search for personal and relational healing. A congregation can seem like a safe place in which to hide feelings of shame. But hiding isn't healing, and hidden shame is dangerously correlated with secrets that harm congregations. It is essential that congregational leaders understand more clearly the legacy of painful shame in their own spiritual lives and its insidious damage within their congregations.

Many faith communities teach the doctrine of shame, often without knowing it. You may have been raised in such a congregation. For example, a core shame message in many Christian congregations is that you must be like Jesus at all times; anything less than that and you have failed. You just don't measure up. You will never be good enough. These are the messages that people with shame are used to hearing. They feel at home with messages sent out from the pulpit, the newsletter, and worship that reinforce shame. They experience the familiarity of family within such a congregation if their own families of origin perpetuated shame. People with shame find shame-based congregations, because they are accustomed to being preached *to*, having fingers pointed in their direction, and the judgment of not measuring up.

MY OWN JOURNEY FROM SHAME TO GRACE

At the time I attended the Jeanne Borsky School of Dance, shame was being taught in the church I was raised in, a typical Protestant congregation in the suburbs of Columbus, Ohio. In Sunday school classes, I learned distinctions between "good" children and "bad" children. Shame was the subliminal message of much of the preaching I heard when I grew old enough to join my parents in their pew. Adolescence provided ample opportunity to add to my list of shame experiences, especially since sexual thoughts and feelings were highly likely to lead me "straight to hell," according to the youth director. I was further shamed by the leaders of my denominational region. When I told them I had received God's call to ordained ministry, they shuffled their feet under the board-room table, shook their heads, rolled their eyes, and said that I was sadly mistaken. I was told that women were not suitable inter-preters of God's word. I was categorically dismissed, adding a page to a story I share with many other women who have sensed God's call to ordained ministry.

The call to serve was undeterred. I changed denominations and went to seminary. I left Ohio behind and went to the West Coast to attend a seminary in Berkeley, California, where, accord-ing to my former committee on ministry, heathens lived on the streets and hippies protested the war, smoked dope, and engaged in group sex. I went there much to the chagrin of my local con-gregation. They had preferred Princeton. I had very few expecta-tions, except perhaps to have an adventure and see an ocean, and I was surprised by what I found.

Despite the liberality of the West, professors and seminarians were stuck in patterns of self-defeating shame. Their words and their lives were often incongruent. Sexual issues were not overtly addressed, but students and professors alike participated in the free love movement during the sexual revolution. Instructors taught us to preach shame because they had plenty of it, even as they tried to free themselves from the rigid morals of traditional Christian theologies.

In church history classes it became clear to me that all Abrahamic religions teach shame to enforce moral behavior. The lives of the faithful are monitored and controlled by clerics who use shame to maintain power and status. A common theme among world religions emerged. A significant amount of humili-ation is promoted as the necessary emotional state leading to re-demption. I lived within an ancient tradition covering thousands of years and a seminary community steeped in secrets and shame. It felt strangely familiar.

Once I was ordained I believed that I could throw off my shame by working hard, putting in long hours and exhausting myself in the effort to lead people to God. I presented myself to the congregation as a person with her act together, but inside I had my doubts. I found comfort in Peter Bohler's instructions to John Wesley when he was a student preacher: "Preach faith until you have it, and then because you have it, you will preach it."[1] This spoke to my shame about my lack of many things, including faith. It provided a word of grace and encouragement I had not often heard in other places along my journey into parish leadership.

As a parish pastor I served several congregations where nearly everyone in them felt ashamed. Some of those congregations had been permanently damaged by shame-bound leaders. Most of them had toxic secrets in them. Others had simply lost their way over time. Members had negative thoughts and feelings about their own congregations. Perhaps the congregation wasn't growing as fast as the congregations around them, they weren't being a moral voice for the community, or they didn't have it in them to create anything new. They were weary of the effort of being Christian in a more and more secular society and shared a deep sense of unworthiness. I reminded them, and myself, of Jesus words: "I came that they may have life, and have it abundantly" (John 10:10). We had such a hard time believing it! I knew intuitively that I had to get free of shame, and that freeing the congregation from shame would make it possible for them to survive, and thrive, for generations to come.

I'd like to tell you that I had a great second conversion at this point in my life, like the author of the hymn "Amazing Grace," who turned his slave ship around and returned his captives to Africa, or like John Wesley, who in the dark hold of a boat was convicted of his lack of faith and went searching for new beliefs. I wish I could tell you that I experienced a still small voice or a near-death experience or a flash of bright light and an apparition of Jesus standing with me on a mountaintop. But none of that happened. I have a life as ordinary as many other people. Grace came

to me gently and slowly in the ordinary experience of a relationship that went badly and the bereavement of my parents' deaths.
The healing began when I decided to no longer carry our shame-
filled family secrets, when I had the chance to start my life over
in a new location, and in those days of weeping in my therapist's
office while she held the space for my healing. God makes change
possible by intervening for us and working within us.

They say that preachers preach what we need to hear, and so
it was a blessing that I had to come up with a sermon every week.
I hauled out every text in the Bible about grace. And I discovered
a Jesus I had not met before. I found a grace-full teacher who not
only was compassionate but who also found delight and joy in our
companionship. John the Baptist said of Jesus, "From his fullness
we have all received, grace upon grace" (John 1:16). Grace began
pouring forth on me.

Once I learned true grace from the inside out, I found that
loving relationships were all around me. Perhaps the prodigal son
had time to think about this while slopping cornhusks for pigs.
The Scriptures say that he "came to himself"; he woke up to the
idea that if he could go home and accept his father's love, he
could also accept himself. Acceptance replaced unworthiness.
Self- and other-acceptance became the norm. Heaviness of heart
was replaced with a lightness of spirit. I picture him coming home
eagerly, and in his father's tearful embrace dancing round and
round in tipsy giddiness. Spontaneity, the ability to accept an embrace, the gratitude of a welcome home to oneself and others all
follow recovery from shame. It's what lies ahead for you and for
your congregation as you read this book.

HERE'S WHERE WE'RE HEADED

You are hereby invited to become a shame-less leader in order to
assist others in your congregational system to find a life of grace.
I am writing *Shame-less Lives, Grace-full Congregations* to teach you
to heal the shame you have likely been carrying around for far

too long. This shame may be rooted in childhood when you experienced parental disapproval or abuse. It may have come into your life as a result of sexual experimentation in your teens or young adulthood. It may have followed a marriage that ended or a relationship in which you carried secrets. It may be that you have taken responsibility for someone else's shame and made it your own.

In this book, I will tell lots of stories about the ways that shame-laden leaders interact with their congregations and ways that congregational shame influences clergy and laity within the "family" system. The faith community you participate in needs your help in creating a place of joy and grace. To do this, you will learn to recognize and heal the shame of your own upbringing, to recognize shame in the behavior of other leaders and clergy around you, to reduce shame-reinforcing theology, and to provide alternative messages of hope and healing. I am convinced that shame-less leaders create shame-less congregations.

I am purposefully playing with the word *shame-less* in the title of this book, since the word *shameless* is usually used in a negative way. My grandmother, for instance, used to say of a woman she knew, "She's a shameless hussy!" We might describe someone who is morally corrupt as shameless. I propose that we reduce (though we likely cannot eliminate) shame and that our best aim is to become shame-less. This is a book to teach you to lessen the shame in your own life and in your relationships.

Throughout the book I describe shame's many forms and disguises. You'll be asked to consider your own shame and will be provided with ways to gently move beyond it. With storytelling and humor, I will bring some of the habits of shame-bound leaders to light so that you gain new insights from those experiences. The book contains examples of many types of shame that erode individual and systemic health, including perfectionism, comparison shame, chronic illness and addiction shame, sexual shame, and pervasive shame. Throughout the book I offer ways to address shame messages and behaviors that have become systemic and habitual in congregational systems. By the end of the book you'll be prepared to overcome shame's emotional gridlock by changing thinking and response patterns.

According to the apostle Paul, we have inherited the immeasurable riches of grace. Jesus has pleasurably lavished grace on us (Eph. 1:5–10). While many church growth experts have been trying to fix the problems of declining congregations, weary leaders who spend time and money examining their inadequacies may increase debilitating shame. The longer our list of failures grows, the more we get locked into a core belief that we are incapable of doing anything differently. Very few authors have taken the step of looking underneath the rocks for the affect of shame. This book is about an emotional adjustment by congregational leaders that will first entail shame consciousness replaced by intentional grace.

In worship one morning, members of the choir, dressed in their beautiful robes, processed into the chancel area, shuffled into place so that everyone could see the director, and after hearing their pitch, began to sing. The women in the front row started singing the melody and the men in the back row came in, but they were obviously not in sync. As they plowed ahead for a few bars, their faces became flushed and distorted, their shoulders drooped, and their breathing grew shallow. The choir director waved her hands to stop the pianist and looked up at them. The choir members all held their breaths like children about to be scolded. What would she say? This could have been a moment for shame. She might have sighed and said, "Let's try again," exposing her frustration and their failure. Instead she said, "I want to start over, because I have heard you sing this song *beautifully*." They stood up taller, they breathed more deeply, and when they began again, it went off without a hitch. They were singing from a place of grace. They were led by a grace-based leader. Turn the page and learn how you can become one too.

CHAPTER 1

Where Shame Begins

Most of us are a little skittish about the subject of shame. This became clear to me in the spring following the release of my book *Sexual Shame: An Urgent Call to Healing*. The university where I teach sets up a biannual reception in the bookstore for faculty who have recently published books, and I was proud to attend the event. My book was prominently placed on a large round table in the center of the room among other offerings such as *A Nature Notes Sampler* and *Golf for the Fun of It*. I watched people walk along the tables where the books were displayed and brush their hands over the covers. Books of poetry, history, and anthropology were lovingly caressed. One of my colleagues picked up the golf book and said he was sending it to his uncle Bob for his birthday. Professors chatted with other authors and offered congratulations.

I stood silently near my book on the table and observed my colleagues. When they came to my book on shame, they stepped back, took their hands off the table, and walked on by. No questions. No comments. The title was bold, the subject bold, and who would want to stand among colleagues with a book on shame in your hands? It might have said something untoward about you or cast a shadow over your otherwise respectable persona. Even the thought of holding such a book seemed to evoke shame.

I am not the first author on the subject to meet with such resistance. Michigan State professor Gershen Kaufman wrote an excellent book, *The Psychology of Shame,* in which he discusses the problem of getting people to take a look at shame. He surmises that the reason authors have shied away from the subject of shame is ironically that there is "a significant degree of shame about shame."[1]

So perhaps we could begin by congratulating ourselves— me, for writing this book, and you, for buying and now reading it. The goal of our undertaking is to find a life with less shame and more grace. To do this, we must brush against the residue of shame in our own lives and endure the discomfort of that experience. While the subject of shame creates anxiety, it can also bring us to a place of grace. My intention is to provide you with enough safety to explore and dissolve the residue of your shame. Once you experience, identify, and become familiar with both shame and grace, you can more confidently love yourself and others.

WHAT EXACTLY IS SHAME?

Shame is a theological and psychological emotion. I define shame as *a feeling of unworthiness in the sight of God or significant others.* In a two-part television special on men who were sexually abused as children, Oprah Winfrey, the program's host, described the feeling of unworthiness that lingers for years beyond the abuse. She noted that if you feel this deep unworthiness, you are more likely to behave in a way that is consistent with your self-devaluation. She accurately pointed to the residue of shame that haunts abuse survivors. Those who directly experience abuse, those who observe others being abused, and the loved ones of survivors all experience the core affect of shame. (We will explore this type of shame in more depth in a future chapter.) Abuse is one of many experiences that lead people to feel deeply unworthy in the sight of God or significant others. Other childhood encounters also set the stage for a life of shame.

SHAME IN OUR DEVELOPING YEARS

Shame develops along with our self-perception in childhood. Shame appears in the form of thoughts, behaviors, and religious beliefs. If you have an experience that you believe to be sin or to be wrong and others reinforce this belief, you begin to talk harshly to yourself. You may even develop an internal dialogue of self-abuse. You say to yourself, "I can't do anything right" or "I'll never amount to anything." You start repeating phrases you heard from your mother, father, a sibling, or a boss. It's as if you've downloaded this language into your internal hard drive, and it pops up on your screen without filters. Eventually you get into a habit of self shaming. The words have become your own. When shame appears as the self-punishing voice inside your head, this is called *intrapersonal shame*, the shame you place upon yourself.

As we develop our own identities, relationships with parents and then peers provide us with feedback that enhances our self-esteem or reinforces a shame-based self-assessment. When shame passes between people, we call this *interpersonal shame*. Family members and friends help the developing ego by providing us with comments of grace such as, "You did your best," and "It's okay to feel that way." Or, if they focus on our failures and inadequacies, they provide us with doses of shame.

I watched a distracted five-year-old boy wander out into the street where a car was approaching. His mother, who was talking to a friend on the sidewalk, saw the oncoming car and yelled, "STOP!" Luckily, he heard her and stopped in his tracks. But as he watched the car whiz by, his body began shaking and tears ran down his face. His mother went to him and scooped him up into her arms. The little boy stammered, "I'm sorry, Momma!" and she responded soothingly, "It's okay, honey. I'm glad you're safe." She offered him grace. And then she corrected his behavior. "It is important to take Mommy's hand before you step off of the curb, okay? Next time we'll look both ways together and be sure it's safe." The boy became calmer, and as he snuggled against his mother's chest, his sobbing stopped. This is the story of a boy receiving parental correction based in affirmation and love. What the mother demonstrates is the power of grace: the boy feels safe and learns an important new lesson. He'll likely remember this incident, and hopefully next time he will cross safely and earn his mother's admiration.

Let's look at the story from the outset again, this time with a parent who approaches the situation with shame rather than grace. The child steps off the curb, the mother yells, "STOP!" and he stops. The mother goes over to the boy, grabs him by the arm, and roughly hauls him onto the sidewalk. She looks at her friend and shakes her head in disgust and embarrassment. She says to her friend, "See what I mean about him?" She says to the boy, "I've told you a million times to take my hand before you cross the street." He is stunned into silence and then mumbles through some tears, "I'm sorry, Mommy." She talks right over his apology, "I don't know why I take you anywhere; all you do is get into trouble." As the boy looks down, shuffles his feet, and continues to sniffle, he begins to think of himself as a bad boy, and a troublemaker. Wanting his mother's love so badly, he adopts her conclusions about him. This is the power of shame.

The boy's mother may have intended to "teach him a lesson." She likely felt that she had to drive her point home to him to keep him safe. My hunch is that she was raised this way as well. People who were devalued and criticized as children become shame-based in their own parenting. "Shame on you!" a mother says so often that her children grow up feeling utterly incapable of ever winning her love.

From one generation to another people can learn and pass on a shame-based parenting. In a shame-based family system, a child's mistakes are seen as evidence of the character flaws of the child. At Thanksgiving our grandson knocked over his milk and someone in the room said, "What's *wrong* with you?" Immediately his behavior was linked to his personhood. I quickly grabbed a towel to mop it up and retorted, "He's a little boy, and he's going to spill his milk sometimes. It's okay." I could see his panicked face soften and relax.

Picture a child with her arm up to her elbow in the cookie jar. "You should be ashamed of yourself!" her father says, hearing the voice of his own father in his head. The little girl who was stealing a cookie from a cookie jar was engaging in a perfectly natural thing to do, but her shame-based father saw it as proof that she was a bad child. A parent working from shame will add this incident to an invisible list of incidents that lead to labeling such a child as *spoiled* or *selfish*. She just wants a cookie; her desire is understandable, and it isn't a character flaw.

THE LOOK OF SHAME

The little boy crossing the street and the little girl with her arm in the cookie jar were visibly distressed. Their faces turned red, they looked down at the ground rather than making eye contact, and their shoulders slouched slightly forward. An astute observer can see shame in the body posture and facial expressions of both children and adults. The closest e-mail emoticon for shame is "embarrassed"—a little round face that's red with blushing. Shame is a strong form of embarrassment, expressed with blushing, downcast eyes, looking away. But in some cultures, downcast eyes and looking away are also signs of respect from one person to another. Loss of eye contact may indicate shame, but it may also indicate honor toward others. Considering the cultural context of a person's posture and downcast gaze, however, we can learn to recognize the affect of shame in others.

Sometimes the signs of shame are subtle, but they can also be obvious. In my counseling office, I have a chair facing the one I sit in. A new client came in and sat sideways in the chair with his legs over the arm of it. As he spoke, he looked at the wall rather than at me. He had a painful secret about which he carried a weight of shame and literally could not face the possibility of my judgment.

His own self-condemnation was so harsh he could not risk receiving any more of it from me. As pieces of the story emerged, I offered compassion. For almost a month, I watched as he gradually turned his body toward me and at last made eye contact. The safer he felt, the more he could let me "see" him. His shame dissolved as he trusted my offerings of grace.

Shame is often referred to as a negative emotion. Psychologists call it an *affect*. It's an uncomfortable emotion, like anger, sadness, and fear. Yet every emotion has a good purpose and exists within the psyche to prompt us toward wholeness. When we feel shame, we need to go to the depths of it to find the core experience and message within it. Our task is to figure out whether the shame fits the crime. Perhaps it is an old feeling that has attached to a current experience. We need to double-check that we're not just repeating the incrimination someone from our past once leveled on us. Is this situation truly worth these feelings of shame? We might ask whether we have said or done something that directly impugns our character or this was a behavioral mistake we can correct. Have we wounded ourselves or others beyond repair?

While shame is uncomfortable and can be debilitating, it can also provide us with information that leads to change. To remain in a place of self-incrimination is life-limiting. To live with daily disgust for others is also life-limiting. The feeling of shame awakens us to a process of discovery. It can move us toward intrapersonal and interpersonal compassion. We can discover shame's opposites, which are acceptance, affirmation, and grace.

The English language has limited ways to explain and define shame. We have but one word to describe both internalized shame (*intrapersonal*) and the shame of others (*interpersonal*). While the intrapersonal experience of shame can be a wake-up call to increase our self-love and acceptance, interpersonal shame serves only to isolate and stigmatize others. Following a lecture on communication between men and women, one of the speakers was challenged by an audience member who criticized him in the form of a question. The lecturer said, "I don't give you permission to shame me today," and went on to the next question. His blunt comment reminded the audience that shaming one another is painful and useless behavior.

Some theorists suggest that shame is necessary in a just and reasonable society and that it keeps us all from running amok. I argue that the only good reason to experience the affect of shame is that the feeling motivates us to explore it and eliminate it. Shaming ourselves or others serves no good purpose.

Some people insist, however, that we *need* to feel shame. When I told a colleague about the title of this book, she said, "I know some shameless pastors!" She meant, of course, that since they have too little shame, they harm congregations by crossing sexual boundaries, by their ego-driven leadership, and through various forms of ineptitude. The problem is not that they have too little shame; it's that they have too much shame and too little grace. I believe that individuals who repeatedly harm themselves and others need grace in order to behave differently. The fact that they have *too much shame* is what leads them to shame-based behaviors. If they feel like they can never measure up, if they feel like no one will accept them no matter what they do, then they are more likely to engage in harmful behavior.

My colleague was also echoing an old belief that people without shame are dangerous. This is based on an idea that was perpetuated by ignorance within the fields of psychology and criminology. People have long thought that without shame, people become psychopathic. We fear the person who is without shame. Yet advances in psychology are finally moving us beyond shaming those without shame. The journey into psychopathology usually begins with multigenerational neglect and abuse, too much shame rather than too little of it, and genetics. More dangerous than a lack of shame is an impaired cognitive ability to understand the consequences of behavior. New studies in neurobiology have identified that some individuals lack what are called *mirror neurons* in the brain. These cells allow us to perceive and actually feel the feelings of others. People who lack sufficient mirror neurons may not have the capacity to relate to the emotional pain of others. Neurobiology is uncovering information that suggests a whole new approach to the question of moral consciousness. We are beginning to cast off the fear that a shameless life will lead to terrible consequences. We can also cast off the old notion that shame is a necessary emotion to ensure right behavior. Replacing shame with grace allows space in the psyche to see oneself differently. Actions can then spring from a place of self-love and lead to respectful relationships with others.

How Guilt and Shame Differ

I make an important distinction between guilt and shame. I believe guilt is the moral compass and the corrective function in the psyche that leads us to notice when we have harmed others with our behavior. Shame, however, is the emotion of self-recrimination that is more likely to weigh us down than spur us to action. We often confuse guilt and shame, but they are not interchangeable words. They are two separate emotions.

The other day when I was running a little late for a class I was teaching at the university, I arrived at a drive-up coffee shop window at roughly the same time as another car. I sped up slightly to get in line before the other driver. As the barista poured my righteous decaf-soy-half-chocolate mocha, I had time to think about my behavior. The word *cutting* came to mind. I detest cutting, but I had in fact cut in front of the other car at the drive-up window. So I was hit with guilt. In my head I said, "I made a mistake." I paid for my mocha, confessed my sin to the barista, and gave her five dollars to purchase a beverage for the person behind me. She could keep the change. I repaired the breach of my own morality by making up for it. I took the time to repent and to forgive myself with this corrective behavior. This experience, while guilt producing, was not shame producing.

Here is the distinction I make. Guilt is the emotion of conviction. It says, "I made a mistake," and when it hits me, I can usually make a course correction. That's what I did with the coffee drive-through experience. I forgave myself and literally moved on. Had

I acted from shame, I would have been less likely to make amends. I would have lambasted myself for running late, barked at the barista, and found a way to blame the person in line behind me for showing up at the same time I got there. If shame had been my leading emotion, my negative self-talk would have sent me spinning off into a chain of verbal self-criticisms.

Sometimes the mistake is larger than my coffee crime and needs to be carefully studied, addressed in therapy, or taken to confession before I can see my way to change it. During grief, people may struggle with guilt and need to find ways to forgive themselves for the way they treated those who have died. Divorce is also a time when people experience guilty feelings, leading them to reflect on the nature of the relationships they have had and how they handled them. This work includes repairing negative self-evaluations. We make mistakes in relationships, we hurt others, and we find ourselves in pain. We cross our own internal value systems and may think, "Why did I do that?" "I knew better!" This is the voice of guilt, which can lead to change and restore us to a positive view of ourselves.

When we hurt someone, guilt is the reminder that a course correction is needed. We feel the sting of the "Oh, no!" or maybe "Oops," and then we prepare the apology. When we acknowledge our mistakes and are sincere in our repentance, we are likely to be forgiven. The goal of guilt, repentance, and forgiveness is a restored relationship. Usually, when the relationship is restored, we also repair the damage inside ourselves. With humility, we face our guilt and address it, which makes us more loving people. At the end of the process, we can breathe more easily, stand tall, and say to ourselves, "Good job getting back on track."

I can tell you that I haven't cut in front of someone at a drive-up coffee shop window since the day I cut off that driver. The experience improved my behavior. Guilt can motivate a change for the better. I know myself to be a kind person. I live by the precepts of Micah 6:8, doing justice and loving kindness and walking humbly with God. The pain that I felt (right after the triumph of pulling ahead and getting my coffee that morning!)

was a reminder of my own value system. I corrected my course, and it's done.

Shame is not a course-correcting emotion. While guilt says, "I *made* a mistake," shame says, "I *am* a mistake." Shame takes a behavior and slaps it onto my core personhood. I become my mistakes. If the above experience had created shame and I had added it to my long list of reasons to conclude that I'm no good, the content would have gone from "I made a mistake" to "I am a mistake." The voice inside my head (that sounds ever so like a parental voice) would still be saying, "Shame on you," and my spiritual superego would have added this experience to a list of my "sins" to remind me that I have once again fallen short of the glory of God. I can picture St. Peter standing in heaven with a long quill pen, shaking his head, making a tut-tut sound. "Ah, cutting in line at a drive-through. Tut-tut." One less chance of getting through the pearly gates for me!

LABELING

Shame has a way of adding every mistake to a list of shortcomings in our souls. The list is more or less invisible most of the time, but occasionally the whole thing appears. Across a lifespan, if you keep a record of every mistake from childhood on, you may end up with a very long list. If every time you make a mistake, the list appears before you, it becomes harder and harder to ignore.

Shame involves labeling oneself or another person as flawed on the basis of one or more "bad" behaviors. A child who takes her time with her homework is labeled lazy by her mother. An uncle calls his nephew a jerk for the way he treats his mom. The child in the grocery store who wants candy at the checkout line is labeled selfish for an ordinary desire for something placed in his path that looks yummy. I could have gone to a place of shame at the drive-up coffee shop window if in my head I had linked my behavior to my character, if I had labeled myself with some words I can't print here. With shame, we use any bad behavior as proof of unworthiness. We engage in our own character assassination.

People who make a long list of their sins eventually conclude that they are not good people making mistakes; they are indeed bad people. Loaded with a good deal of shame, they feel unworthy to the core. They feel unredeemable because of unacceptable thoughts, feelings, or experiences. Throughout the book I will be referring to these people as *shame-bound*. The term describes a fixed pattern of self-shaming cognitions that limit growth and lower self-esteem.

Shame-bound people may have learned to loathe themselves early in life. They are told that if they spill their milk, it's because they are bad children (too wiggly, too distracted, clumsy, and so forth). A child who resists chores (don't we all?) is told that he is lazy, rather than being honored for wanting a more laid-back and playful life. You've heard a parent in a restaurant say to a child who is noisy, "I can't take you anywhere; you are such a bad girl."

Sandra decided to finally face years of being told that every bad action confirmed her inadequacy. Sandra's parents had used Bible verses to chastise her and frightened her with images of hell-fire and eternal damnation. Sandra became frozen with fear in her early twenties. She saw every decision as "right" or "wrong" and constantly worried about making the "right" decision. For Sandra, the task of trying to be good took over all else and kept her in perpetual striving. She had an ordinary number of problems in her life, she had made mistakes and learned from them, but she could not hold on to the idea of grace. Sandra saw herself as worse than everyone else and incapable of growth and insight. Sandra was shame-bound. She viewed her problems as created by her inadequacy, and everything she learned from mistakes was overshadowed by her statement, "I should have known better in the first place." Every decision she had to make was extremely painful.

Rather than ask, "What did I learn from this?" a person raised with shame asks, "Was I right or wrong?" In its most debilitating form, the thinking pattern in which every behavior is good or bad, right or wrong, a success or a failure leads to what psychologists define as obsessive thinking. The mind ruminates for hours and weeks about every decision. The ruminations are a psychological strategy used to avoid suffering the weight of shame that can follow a perceived wrong decision.

Many of us grew up in families where behaviors were labeled as right or wrong, and found faith communities with theological belief systems that reinforced dichotomous thinking. Some preachers will proclaim that every decision you make in life can be evaluated by whether or not the Bible says it's good or bad. The lack of middle ground in any philosophical or theological teaching leads the person with shame into a debilitating fixation on doing the "right" thing.

Congregations often unknowingly reinforced shame. As children we learn to sing, "Jesus loves me this I know, for the Bible tells me so," but by the time we get to youth group we are singing, "Shackled by a heavy burden, 'neath a load of guilt and shame," and eventually we grow into, "There is a balm in Gilead, to heal the sin-sick soul." Given sufficient doses of shame at various developmental stages, people become shame-bound and feel that heavy burden of sin upon them almost constantly. This burden, they are told at church, is helpful and necessary for their salvation. Nothing could be further from the truth.

People who are dosed with shame have an even harder time grasping the message of salvation. As shame is reinforced by the actions of members and leaders of congregations, individuals are less likely to receive and believe the gospel of grace. In one congregation, the young single woman who became pregnant was shamed by not being invited to the annual shower for new mothers. This deepened her disappointment in herself and increased her negative self-talk: "I'm just a slut." When congregants whispered behind her back and called her baby illegitimate, she became bitter and disconnected from God. This made it less likely for her to be sure of her salvation. Shame leads us to more shame; it doesn't lead us to grace.

People in most congregations endure messages about their unworthiness on any given Sunday. Although some of these messages are sent out unintentionally, nevertheless, parishioners learn to connect the dots. When a pastor talked with her congregation about adding a new service with communion every Sunday, a parishioner sought her out. "I don't need communion every Sunday," the member said, "because I don't sin that much!" She saw communion solely as a ritual for cleansing.

She didn't pull that idea out of the air. Traditional language around the communion ritual in many denominations includes a line that says something like, "We are unworthy to come to the table." As the pastor prepares to preach she says, "May the words of my mouth and the meditations of our hearts be acceptable in thy sight . . ." This can be heard as a blessing or a warning, depending on your level of shame. The person with shame may hear this as a warning that God will not accept some of the meditations of our hearts. It could be heard to imply that we are unacceptable in God's sight unless our meditations are "right." We may not be good enough to rightly receive the word this morning. Maybe the preacher isn't good enough either! What if, instead, the preacher said, "May the words of my mouth and the meditations of our hearts join with the intention of your holy spirit for our growth and grace, O Lord, our rock and our redeemer."

If we lean into grace, we know we are acceptable and beloved. Believing this, our words and our thoughts will be full of God's loving intention.

JESUS AND THE LANGUAGE OF GRACE

In Jesus's preaching and teaching he shows us the power of language to create loving and grace-filled relationships. More inclined to remind people of their goodness than their failings, he uplifts and heals those around him. What might our congregations be like if we follow his style of speaking truth *with love* and eliminate our tendencies toward judging labels?

At church we are told that engaging in even one "sin" makes us a "sinner." In a shame-based theology, one bad act can result in eternal damnation, especially if it's a sexual act. In a workshop for clergy on sexual abuse prevention, a participant loaned me his hand-drawn picture of the ladder of fornication that he had been given by his Sunday school teacher. Remember singing "We Are Climbing Jacob's Ladder"? In this old song, you get the feeling that right actions will get you to heaven for eternity. But with the ladder of fornication, rather than rise to heaven like Jacob, we descend straight down into hell, one kiss, one embrace, one incident of touching someone under clothing—and so on and so forth—one step at a time. Too many congregations have preached and taught that when it comes to sex, even one bad thought can put you at risk. "Bad" sexual behavior equals "bad" person. Sin equals sinner.

Jesus of the Gospels pays more attention to mercy than to sin. He teaches the scribes and Pharisees that healing may result from changed behavior as well as forgiven sin. He challenges those who judge others saying, "Let anyone among you who is without sin be the first to throw a stone at her" (John 8:7b), and only in a few contexts is he quoted using the term *sinners*. For example, we read, "Those who are well have no need of a physician, but those who are sick; I have come to call not the righteous but sinners to repentance" (Luke 5:31–32). In this story, the tax collector's humility brought him into the light of Christ. Along with Levi, we are invited to turn toward wellness and the physician, who can restore us. The emphasis in the story is on the graciousness of God's healing rather than Levi's faults.

Jesus is a shame-free preacher. He leads by example, and his parables direct us to a life of grace. Early in Luke's Gospel, we find Jesus preaching to the crowds at the lakeshore where many came "to hear him and to be healed of their diseases" (Luke 6:18). He asks his followers to do more than simply love those who love them back and not to lend only to those who lend in return. He notes that "even sinners" do these things. You, who are *not* sinners, he implies, should "love your enemies, do good, and lend expecting nothing in return." He asks them to think of themselves more highly than sinners, to love without reserve (Luke 6:32–35).

In a teaching on the danger of judging, Jesus asks his followers to be gracious toward others and to consider their tendency to blame and condemn (Luke 13:2). He also compares a sinner to a lost sheep, saying that the heavens are full of rejoicing when the wandering one is found (Luke 15:7, 10). In this instance, Jesus's use of the word *sinner* comes in the context of a call to utter love, an emphasis on the restoration of right relationships. In the story of the blind man from John's Gospel, Jesus is asked to assign fault and refuses to do so (John 9:1–7). He more often liberates than condemns. He avoids labeling.

One might ask why the term *sinner* has been so pervasive in Christian theology. Psychology suggests that we project onto others what we disown in our own hearts. The habit of placing judgment on sinners keeps us at a safe distance from them. We shame ourselves when we use the term *sinner,* as well. We are, by this term, creating distance from God and others rather than drawing nearer. The term has been lifted from the Scriptures and flung about by pious and self-righteous theologians and congregational leaders. I will avoid flinging it back, but I need to say that the term has been too often overused and misused. We can do well without it.

Taking Someone Else's Inventory

In the recovery programs of Alcoholics Anonymous, people are asked to make a fearless inventory of the consequences of their negative behaviors. They are warned against the mental gymnastics of making up *someone else's* list. And yet congregations have seen it as their duty to judge and label the behavior of others. Roy and Sue attended a congregation where the lay leaders believed that it was their moral duty to talk with them about the precariousness of their salvation. To set them on the right course, these leaders identified and made lists of Roy's "sins" and Sue's "sins," which they handed to Roy and Sue in their living room over a cup of coffee. The lists included character flaws like "selfishness" and "pride." They each had ten to twelve words or sentences on their lists that in effect added layer upon layer of shame. They sat in silence for a while as the coffee grew cold, not knowing how to respond to these people they had considered their friends. Ron and Sue grew silent in humiliation and shame. The visitors left after saying a prayer that Ron and Sue would, by reading these lists, restore their relationship with Christ and the church.

It didn't take long for Roy and Sue to move from humiliation to anger. They had sufficient self-esteem to know that what the church had done to them was spiteful and abusive. After reading the lists a few times and toying with self-criticism, they found the strength to put shame aside and live into the grace of God. They decided that these people were not really friends to have given them those lists, and that they deserved a whole lot better. They raised their heads, they burned the lists, and they left that congregation. Today they are among the humblest and most faithful people you could meet, because they live with "grace upon grace." They grace themselves with acceptance, and they grace each other. They have looked at their own shame and the shaming of others and made a decision to live without it. They no longer think of themselves as sinners. They recognize and celebrate that they are saved by grace.

Our theological ancestors have reinforced shame, partly because they have felt so much of it themselves, and in part to strengthen the argument that Jesus is all powerful. As a child of mainline Protestantism, I was taught that Jesus was so powerful that he could save *even me*—though I was hardly worthy of such a gift. He could exchange my unworthiness for salvation. This theology left me with a niggling question. What if, in my case, it didn't take? What if I would go on being unworthy, no matter what salvation provided for everyone else? What if I was *too unworthy*? In music, in liturgy, and in preaching, I heard more messages about my unworthiness than messages about God's delight in me.

Jesus did not teach the message that we should discredit ourselves in order for him to have the glory. Yes, some people obviously think it is up to us to tell a member of the congregation or a neighbor, a friend, or a child that they can't possibly measure up to Jesus's example. They still believe in the power of shame. But it is neither the intent nor the content of Jesus's teachings that we should wallow in unworthiness. Rather, Jesus taught that everyone sins from time to time and that it is what we make of the goodness and wholeness of our lives that matters most. His beckoning love was so compelling that ordinary people left their old lives behind to follow him, not to be redeemed of their sinfulness but because he honored their capacity for loving and serving others. He told them that he had come so that they could find lives of abundant joy. He showed them the healing power of speaking the truth in love, and he healed every physical and emotional sickness with compassion and grace. Contrary to what our theological ancestors might have thought, we don't help him to look or be more powerful by shaming ourselves or by shaming others. We can be shame-less in our approach to God, others, and our own salvation.

As you begin this exploration of shame and grace, consider suspending the use of the term *sinner*. Calling someone else, or yourself, a sinner is a form of verbal abuse. Instead of saying "I'm a sinner," try saying, "I'll take up my bed and walk" just for a while and see what happens. The term *sinner* is insidious verbal battery disguised as religious discipline. Letting go of it will be your first homework assignment as this exploration of shame and grace continues.

CHAPTER 2

Yours, Mine, and Ours
Overlapping Dynamics of Shame

On the Sunday following the repeal of the nation's "Don't ask, don't tell" policy, I found myself in tears because something very dear to me was welling up. Although the policy had sought to protect gay, lesbian, bisexual, and transgendered military personnel, it had in fact closeted them. When the measure was reversed, I felt as if the government gave me permission to tell my family story after years of silence and secrets. I followed the prompting of my emotions and proceeded to write an essay that I soon felt compelled to share with my church family. Following the format of the oral history project StoryCorps, it consisted of excerpts from my father's journal beginning in December 1941 and my responses to his writing. With the bombing of Pearl Harbor, my father's life story took a dramatic turn. He was drafted into the United States Army.

When the United States declared war on Japan, my father was taken away from his world of social interactions at college, a woman he had chosen to marry and raise a family with, and the drama department where he could cut up without repercussions. His sexual orientation wasn't even a conscious question in his mind, since he dated and fell in love with my mother. He was just nineteen years old when he was deployed, and, as is typical

31

for most of us, those years solidified his sexual orientation. My father entered a culture of sexual exploration when he entered the hidden world of sexual relationships between men in the army. He was stationed at a post in a secret underground location in New York City, where he watched for submarines in the channels. Ironically, he was also underground in another way, as he grew clearer and clearer about his romantic and emotional interest in the men around him. He spent years after the war keeping secrets about his military "friends," who were more than likely also his male lovers. Dad was left with shame and ambivalence about his years in the military because they were filled with narratives he couldn't share.

As I reviewed Dad's stories about those years, I was flooded with feelings. I had inherited my father's shame about being a gay man who served in the military. His shame had become mine. But why would *I* carry shame about this? Sometimes we carry shame without conscious knowledge of it. Shame is as subtle as second-hand smoke and can be as deadly. I didn't go looking for shame to pick up and carry forward for my father and didn't know I was carrying this burden for his years in the military. But I have learned to notice when strong feelings arise and then to go looking for what students of science, history, and theology call source material. I have learned to examine the nature of my feelings and their originating causes. When Congress repealed "Don't ask, don't tell," I went looking for source material.

When my father returned home from the war, he took my mother in his arms, danced her around the USO hall, and married her. My sister and I came along and grew up assuming life in the family was normal, as most of us assume about our families. I had a vague feeling, however, that something wasn't quite right.

When I was a teenager, Mother and I would pull books of family photographs off the shelf and sit next to each other on the couch to look through them. The sepia-toned pictures in black mounting corners helped us mark the transitions of our lives and the passing of time. We engaged in this ritual on holidays and later whenever I returned home from college. It brought us closer together because it provided a way for mother to tell me what she could about her life.

When we opened a large grey book to a page with pictures from what mom called "the war years," I asked her, "Who's the handsome guy here with Dad?" Their T-shirt sleeves were rolled up, and they were puffing on cigarettes. The man's hair was shining black, and he had his right arm casually draped around my father. They were both smiling, standing in front of their pup tent at boot camp. Mother dodged my question, as she often did, with the comment, "Oh, you don't want to know that." My mother's avoidance was part and parcel to her shame. It was a clue, but not one I understood at the time.

I made another unconscious attempt to uncover my father's story in young adulthood by working in chaplaincy with gay men and their health-care providers during the AIDS epidemic in Northern California in the eighties. I found myself drawn inexplicably into the world of gay men. Without obvious explanation, I picked up and read freelance reporter Randy Shilts's book *Conduct Unbecoming*, about the careers and oppression of gays and lesbians in the military. At more than six hundred pages, it's the longest book I've ever devoured, and I was never bored while reading it. It was the closest I could come to understanding my father's experience in the military, but I didn't consciously know why I was so interested in it.

When I was in my midthirties, near the end of my father's life, he disclosed his sexual orientation and claimed his identity as a gay man. At that point, mother began telling the truth, and the shame began to lift. The ambivalence and bitterness my parents had about their forty years of marriage finally made sense. The heavy emotional silence they had carried about my father's military years had been expressed in her comment, "Oh you don't want to know about that." My mother had turned those pages of the photo album as quickly as possible, sometimes skipping several at a time, but curiously no one had removed them from the book. They were a photobiography of an aspect of my father's life they both acknowledged but couldn't speak about.

My reactions to the repeal of "Don't ask, don't tell" indicate the power of shame. If you'd asked me the day before the repeal if I carried lingering shame about my father's military service, I would have said, "I don't think so." I might have said that it wasn't a big deal. If you'd seen the family photo album and asked me who that guy was in the muscle shirt with his arm draped around my young, handsome father, I would have said, "I guess I'll never know." I might have said that it had all happened before I came along. And yet, the day Congress took that vote, an era of ambivalence and shame about my gay father's military service ended. The residue of shame dissipated.

The Healing Benefits of Pride

The following Sunday morning I said, out loud in church, "I feel proud of my gay father." I expressed a sentiment that not even liberal congregations are used to hearing. I wasn't the only person in tears or feeling a little more proud. People in the room who had family members in the service, people who have also lived with secrets for years, people who had kept silent about their loved ones were also given permission to be open about their past. The experience that morning was changing us, replacing shame with honor and respect.

I have experienced the change from shame to pride and watched it take place with others in my roles as pastor and psychotherapist. Once the stigma is gone and the shame lifts, there is a perceptible difference in how we feel, how tall we stand, how deeply we laugh. Telling my congregation about my father's life as a gay man in the military, I felt like the child of an alcoholic parent standing in a circle of other children of alcoholics and proclaiming, "I didn't create it, but I carried the weight of it for years!" The universal need that touched the congregation that morning was for all of us to replace shame with honor and pride. In the days and weeks that followed, people revealed stories to me about their gay father, uncle, sister, grandfather, and son. Just as I had said I was proud of my father and our country, they expressed their pride in their loved ones, the kind of pride that is not a deadly sin but rather a celebration of a loved one's life.

This feeling of newfound pride can present a real dilemma to us, because many of us have been warned since childhood about the dangers of pride. In traditional Catholicism, pride is viewed as a cardinal sin. It is at the top of the list of the seven deadly sins, because it is believed to be the most ungodly of them all. In Protestant Sunday school, I was told that pride is the opposite of humility. Too often, though, a lack of pride is humiliation.

Teachings on pride date back to early Christianity, where it appears in a list of eight cardinal sins known as *logismo,* compiled, as best we know, by Saint John Cassian (360–435). Others have attributed the list to Evagrius of Pontus, a Greek Christian from about that era. Scholars agree that it was refined by Pope Saint Gregory the Great (590–640). You don't have to be Catholic to know about this list of seven deadly sins. Although the sins are never specifically listed in the Bible, throughout all of Christendom preachers and theologians have used the list to identify those sins that are most pernicious. Pride, they believed, leads to all of the others. Thomas Aquinas, for example, noted that "self-love is the cause of every sin."[1]

Scriptural texts about the problem of pride are found in Proverbs (8:13, 11:2, 13:10, 16:18, 29:23) with a few references in Isaiah (14:12–15, 22). The Gospels contain no direct references to pride. Jesus does not specifically condemn it, and in fact, he raises the esteem and pride of those whom he encounters. In his encounter with the Samaritan woman, for example, he lifted her out of shame by offering her a nonjudgmental opportunity to change her behaviors. After her encounter with him, she returned to her community to convert them to Christ. To do that, she had to set aside their condemnation of her and replace her low self-esteem with pride in her own capacity to change. Only then could she give her life for the benefit of others. Indeed, the Samaritan woman teaches us that replacing shame with pride is essential. She could not have left her old life behind her without a feeling that someone, in this case Jesus, would be proud of her change. Her growing sense of self-esteem was a necessary catalyst for her changed life and her life in service to others. I doubt that Jesus worried about her getting a swelled head or becoming egotistically dangerous.

When pride becomes a belief in one's superiority, it can be truly quite harmful. We can see inordinate amounts of pride leading to entitlement, objectification, moral superiority, and class and race prejudice. This has been an appropriate concern for clergy and congregations. We could benefit from having two words to describe pride: one for the ego run amok with its own self-aggrandizement that Thomas Aquinas warned about and the other for the healthy and necessary esteem that counteracts shame and humiliation. It was healthy and necessary esteem that the Samaritan woman found in the eyes of her loving Lord. If we had a word for positive pride, we could remove pride from the list of grave sins.

Emphasis on dangerous aspects of pride has likely been rooted in the desire of those in power to retain that power. Patriarchal interpreters of Scripture have justified their right to amass wealth, to tell others the true meaning of the gospel, and to define right behavior and wrong behavior in order to keep others "in their place." Theologians have suggested that if humanity raises itself up too high, it could falsely claim to be godlike and in the end attempt to replace God as supreme. The story of the Tower of Babel has often been used as a reminder of the dangers of pride. Those who wish to maintain a superior position, theology, or status tell the people around them to beware of pride.

Prideful behaviors may or may not be considered sinful depending on who is engaging in them. Believing in one's superiority and expressing those beliefs is viewed differently depending on gender. Women are told not to think too highly of themselves. This keeps them feeling inferior to the men around them and inferior to male leaders in congregations. Women are told to humble themselves. A prideful woman has been seen as a bane to her partner, her family, and her peers. A prideful man is seen to possess leadership qualities, to be righteous, and to take his rightful place as the head of his family. He is thought of as having the qualities of a good civic leader and politician. We will overlook the "sin" of his high level of self-regard and regard him well too. We accept his pride and expect it to take him a long way in life. This gender difference in the labeling and condemning of others adds to my insistence that pride is a complicated and unfairly distributed "sin."

While we might want to write off pride as an outdated construct of an ancient culture and time, research and commentary about the seven deadly sins continues. In the late 1990s, researchers at Kansas State University's department of geography mapped the United States on the basis of the prevalence of each of the deadly sins in that state. States with the greatest pride were determined by adding up the lust, gluttony, greed, sloth, wrath, and envy within them. Pride was considered the most heinous sin of them all.[2]

Healthy Pride

While contemporary culture is not likely to let go of its suspicion about pride, psychology and grace-based theology can assert the necessity of pride in gaining esteem and overcoming shame. We need to feel proud of ourselves and to encourage others in developing healthy pride. People who feel proud of themselves are more likely to attract nonabusive mates. A battered woman needs to know that she is a person of worth and have enough pride to stop verbal battery by those around her. People who feel capable of great achievements (that is, who have sufficient pride) take necessary risks that lead them to great success.

We also need others around us to feel and express their pride in us. While my mother often casually told me how proud she was of me, the two times that my father told me he was proud of me are seared into my memory and fill my heart with great gratitude. Children need to hear their parents tell them that they are worthy and esteemed. This helps them develop a core positive sense of self. A friend of mine used the nickname Rob throughout his life.

When someone asked why he didn't use his formal name, Robert, he said, "Because when I hear my nickname, I hear my father's proud voice saying, "At-a-boy, Rob."

Pride is helpful and life giving to the human soul. In psychology, pride is viewed as synonymous with self-esteem. People with a good deal of shame are especially in need of the corrective emotional experience of pride. When I counsel clients, one of my tasks is to help them to feel proud of themselves. As they grow and change, they also need to pause and notice their success. Their next positive change depends on their interpretation of the last one. Are they proud of it? Did they do well in confronting a boss, in making a decision, in taking care of themselves when they needed to? If so, they are likely to repeat those experiences. As children of God, they can be proud of their ability to love and be loved, that they are bright, skilled, and accomplished. They have permission to feel proud.

We all need to feel good about ourselves, our families, and our accomplishments. Unfortunately, feelings of healthy pride are missing when there are secrets and shame in family systems. In my counseling practice I watch people become more confident, make desired changes, and do courageous things. Sadly, as some of them grow stronger and start to feel more capable, they are hit by their own resistance to happiness. A wave of shame comes over them for feeling proud. This is such a no-win situation. If they keep the shame, they can avoid the "sin" of pride. If they let go of the shame, then they end up with pride, which they were told by their families or preachers is a serious offense.

In a dysfunctional family, children are not given permission to feel proud of themselves. They are told things like, "Don't get a swelled head" and "You shouldn't think too highly of yourself!" They are discouraged from feeling successful or superior, because this might lead them into narcissistic pride. In some cases, this attitude totally blocks their ability to grow more self-assured, assert themselves in abusive situations, or take up a new life journey that could provide them with joy and healing.

To eradicate shame, we have to allow healthy pride back into our self-perceptions and allow others around us to feel pride too. We become frightened of this idea, however, if we have been harmed by someone's overly prideful or narcissistic self-presentation. The person with narcissism has, at his or her core, a shamed self, rather than a prideful self. The person who has a narcissistic personality disorder has pulled a mask of righteousness over a core belief that the interior self is unworthy. This person has too much shame, masked by too much pride.

While the damage of thinking too highly of ourselves is clearly evident in the abuse of power, sense of entitlement, use of others for personal gain, and false benefit of being revered by others, the damage of thinking too poorly of ourselves also has to be explored and addressed. Thinking too little of ourselves keeps us locked in victimization, learned helplessness, and shame. Too much shame can be overcome with healthy pride. Dignity and respect can undo the dangerous legacy of shame inside a personality, family, or organizational system.

INHERITABLE SHAME

I am not the only daughter who has carried a parent's shame. We carry shame for our parents because we are good at helping them deal with their negative feelings. As children we learn to mimic their feelings, and we also have a tendency to feel feelings that our parents disown. We may unconsciously try to help an ashamed parent by feeling similarly. We take on the shame that surrounds family secrets without even knowing what those secrets are.

We are learning through advances in science that our feelings have genetic components. We may literally inherit the emotional landscapes of our parent. New research in neurobiology is proving that people's traumatic experiences alter their brains in several ways, including their ability to regulate and manage emotions. With advanced imaging these changes can now be seen in subsequent generations. Family experiences such as child sexual abuse, sudden death, abandonment, witnessing abuse, and physical violence of any kind can cause a child to inherit shame. When secrets surround the experience, the shame grows stronger.

Clients who come into my counseling practice quite often indicate that they would prefer not to look back over their history and their family stories. This may be due to lingering shame about feelings, thoughts, or experiences. This actually indicates the power of their life narrative and feelings they presume to have left behind. They may even say that they have worked through issues from their past in therapy, but my immediate question is, if that is true, why avoid them now?

My best promise is that the client and I will go back there only if the present day seems to be stuck in the past. We will go there to get unstuck. We will have to look backward if the client has borrowed or inherited feelings from parents that interfere with emotions or behaviors in the current day. We will find and examine old feelings that linger below the surface. While many emotions of the past can be roadblocks in the present, shame is the emotion that particularly likes to stay in hiding. A conscious life is worth reviewing for signs of shame. The goal is to examine and reduce that shame so that we become shame-less. It may not be as difficult or as painful as our fears suggest.

THE PERSONAL AND INTERPERSONAL OVERLAP

The interplay between our feelings of shame and shame in the systems in which we participate is quite complex. As clergy and lay leaders play various roles in the congregational system, we must be aware that we have learned those roles in our families of origin. The shame we learned in childhood will likely be replicated in the congregational context. As Rabbi Edwin H. Friedman wrote in his classic work *Generation to Generation: Family Process in Church and Synagogue,* the emotional dynamics of our families of origin reappear as we participate in religious organizations. He explains,

"The one nonfamily emotional system that comes closest to a personal family's intensity is a church or synagogue, in part because it is made up of families, and in part because so much of the force of religion in realized within the family."[3]

We are inevitably drawn into the emotions of the congregational system because we are, if we remain unconscious of old feelings and projected emotions, still carrying the residue of shame from our families. These overlapping systems are more easily explained through a story of the ways I met up with shame in a declining congregation.

The Guest Preacher

It was early on Sunday morning, and I was the guest preacher at a congregation I had never before attended. Mine was the first car in the parking lot, and it took me awhile to find an unlocked door. After a self-guided tour of the facility, I at last found my way to the sanctuary and the narthex. From the pastor's office, a parishioner emerged with an "I'm in charge here" attitude. Let's call her Edith. Here is how Edith greeted me: "You must be the guest preacher today. Well, I'll tell you, the last time we had a woman preacher, she sat in the wrong place." It would prove to be a long morning. But, hey, I've spent some time in shame recovery, so I said, "Wow! Let's not let that happen again. Let's walk right on in there, and you can show me where to sit." I started down the aisle, and she followed me. She showed me where to sit—in the darkened mahogany straight-backed chair with carved scrollwork. It was obviously built for a large Viking king and brought over on a ship from Norway in the 1800s. No wonder the last person sat somewhere else. I smiled politely. "Okay," I said. I like to be liked, and so I admit it: I gave in.

As Edith and I talked, there appeared three men in their usher suits who were having a serious-sounding conversation. They looked up as Edith and I walked by. Edith said nothing at all. I smiled and said hello, and then added in jest, "Whatever you do, don't move the pews around." They stared. They didn't laugh.

They didn't ask me what I meant by that. They just looked at me blankly, so we walked on. It would be a long morning, as I said.

(I'd like to have told them of several congregations that split apart or died as a result of pew movement. A seminary graduate who arrived in a rural church with a historic sanctuary was eager to try "new" forms of worship. Before his first Sunday, wanting to foster fellowship, he moved all of the pews so they faced each other. How long do you think he lasted? Six months, which is really unusual, because he was Methodist and Methodist bishops make midyear appointments only in extreme cases, such as sexual misconduct, embezzlement, arson—or moving all the pews.)

It was clear that Edith's congregation had not changed anything for many years. As the time for worship grew nearer, about twenty people arrived. Edith and I got down to the business of highlighting which one of us was going to do what. As lay reader, she would handle the usual sections. I got the prayers, the Gospel reading, and the sermon. I had to be kindly persuasive about reading the Gospel myself. I robed up under her watchful gaze and said a prayer alone, because frankly I didn't feel safe offering one with Edith, and then we processed on the opening hymn.

The service went well, from my view up at the prow of the ship. We exited on the last hymn, and on the way out Edith said to me, "Well, I guess we didn't need to say the Lord's Prayer today, since we say it *every other* Sunday!" She sighed so loudly that you could hear her above the singing of the congregation.

What was she thinking? After all, she was up there right next to me with that order of service in front of her; she could have inserted that prayer anywhere she wanted to. Liturgy is the work of the people! How about helping me out? Before leaving, I shook a few hands, got my check from Edith, and vowed never to return.

The Residue

What could we predict about that congregation today? They no longer have a permanent pastor because their budget is too small. The children who were once in Sunday school grew up and departed. The surrounding neighborhood is full of young, diverse, and multicultural families. A school is one block away. But none of those children are drawn into the church for activities or worship. And because of declining giving, the building is unwelcoming and in disrepair.

Is it possible that the attitude of one shame-based leader could disrupt the life of the entire congregation? I am going to boldly say yes, because this woman's shame was extremely contagious, and I saw other signs that shame permeated the system. For example, the ushers had lost their sense of humor, and there were no children to remind the adults that mystery, wonder, and playfulness are at the heart of a faith walk. The congregation had lost the ability to articulate a purpose for existence and lost its passion for evangelism. Members stopped inviting their friends to join them. All of these were signs of shame about what they had to offer. As their sense of scarcity increased, the lay leaders became frightened and bitter. People like Edith martyred themselves to the cause in a dismal situation. Congregational leaders didn't like her behavior, but they needed her.

Edith likely grew up in a shame-based family system. Perhaps her older brother got all of the glory or perhaps she was an outsider in her own family system. Maybe her father abandoned the family when she was very young. Maybe her mother still carried shame about Edith's birth father, even after finding a "good man" and having additional children. Maybe Edith had been sexually abused as a child by a family member or neighbor. I don't know the causes of Edith's rigidity and shame. I don't know what drove her to an overly serious attitude about worship. But I know that for the congregation to survive, someone in the congregational system or some pastor would need to come along and gently, gracefully redirect Edith and teach her to engage in loving behavior. Someone needed to teach Edith about shame in order to heal her and the congregation.

I once read a magazine article (that I have not since been able to locate) that was called something like "The Power of One Bad Waiter." The story traced the simultaneous opening of two restaurants on the same city block. One of them had a waiter who was negative, ignored his customers, and was impatient with their complaints about the food or the service. The restaurant with just one bad waiter was closed within three months of opening. The restaurant with carefully hired, positive staff and a goal of excellent customer service was thriving years after building an enthusiastic clientele.

I encountered one bad waiter in my hometown when a restaurant opened last year. A colleague and I went to lunch there and each ordered a yummy-sounding salad. The waiter brought the salads and one wedge of bread, about two inches across. When I asked who the bread was for (not wanting to eat my friend's bread), he put his hands on his hips, sighed the sigh that means "shame, shame," and told us that we were to share the bread, and if we *needed* more he'd bring us another after that. While I cherish communion, we had not exactly planned on such a ritual over lunch in a café near our offices. We didn't ask for more (we were too ashamed), and we didn't return to the restaurant. Within about nine months, the restaurant had closed. Everyone said it was the location. I said it was one bad waiter.

Edith was the one bad waiter at the congregation where I was the guest preacher. People who encountered her would not likely come back. Only those who had known her for years were able to say, "She's just like that," and ignore her bad behavior. Their tolerance led to a congregation in a terminal condition, and they are likely to close their doors within the year.

It turns out that the larger congregational family system was laden with secrets and shame. Several generations back in this congregation, a pastor had crossed a sexual boundary. This secret and its lingering shame had attracted shame-based leaders and leaders who were comfortable covering up "the bad stuff." The intuitive feeling that "there's something wrong here" might have come over visitors seeking a new church home, turning them away. The same thoughts and feelings may have attracted Edith to the congregation because its shame felt familiar and, in an odd way, comfortable to her. People with healthy pride and self-esteem, people who had healed their lives of their own shame, wouldn't have stayed in that congregation for more than a few Sundays. In the end, the people who remained within the congregation were a little depressed, lacked humor, and stayed there out of habit. A few of them would have been loyal to that congregation no matter what, but they didn't know how to create an ongoing system within which people could rejoice, form community, and find healing.

Congregational systems can become used to shame. They can become so used to it that they don't see it, identify it, or change it. They may never get to the source material for their own church family stories or feelings. They may go along for years as we did in my family of origin, sensing that something is wrong but lacking the skills needed to discover it and heal it. In some ways, Edith was a symptom carrier for the unease in her congregational family system. She was able to play that role because her personal shame overlapped with the shame of the congregation.

Where Grace Disables Shame

The healing of a congregation with immense quantities of shame requires a good deal of intervention. A pastor with an understanding of shame could begin to uncover the root causes of the shame in order to name and eradicate it. The leaders would have to engage in a lively, honest, and creative process of social interaction that lowers shame and increases the esteem of the congregation. They would have to be realistic about the slow and steady decline that results from an overly shamed and shaming congregation. Instead of hanging their heads in self-deprecating verbal criticism, they'd have to see what could yet be made of the situation. If they could be proud of all that was positive in their history, even a congregation that was deeply troubled could either transform their ministry or shame-lessly move toward closure.

To continue as a community of faith, Edith's congregation would set ground rules that clearly spelled out expectations for interpersonal conduct, including respect, acceptance, and

gratitude. Criticism and shame would have to be reduced and replaced with compassion and grace. Once new behavioral ground
rules were in place, they would also need to challenge each other
when old behaviors surfaced. I would assign someone to stand
alongside the congregation's "Edith" (every shame-based congregation has at least one) to welcome new visitors and be sure that
all comments were affirming. She could learn to change her old
habit of shaming and improve her relationships in the congregation as well as at home or work. Asking individuals to address
their shame is essential to creating healthy community. A person
like Edith needs acceptance rather than a laissez-faire attitude
about her bad behavior. But Ediths also need others to challenge
them to change by offering love and grace. If they change and feel
proud of themselves, they will keep on changing and feed positive
energy back into the congregational system. Just as shame begets
shame, grace begets grace.

The Sunday I wrote my coming-out essay about my gay father's
military service was a Sunday when shame fell off quite a few of us.
Part of the grace extended that day came via my phone call to the
pastor to ask her for a few minutes of time during worship. She
said, "Yes, of course. We'll do it at prayer time." I had bumped into
grace. She could have said (and might well have thought), "How
long is it?" or "Will it offend anyone?" or "I think our service is
full, and I hate to run overtime." But she didn't. She allowed for
the spontaneity of personal witness that is at the heart of a lively
Christian community. I'm still attending church, despite plenty
of reasons (such as that old list of seven deadly sins!) to abandon
the whole kit and caboodle. I participate in a congregation where
grace disables shame. When I go there, I am shame-lessly proud of
myself, my family, and them.

CHAPTER 3

We're All Different
Creating Shame-Less
Congregational Cultures

After the war in Vietnam, the Hmong and Mein people of Northern Laos who had fought alongside US soldiers in the war relocated to the United States. They settled in various regions across the country. In a small town in the central valley of California, where I served as pastor, many extended Southeast Asian families arrived in the mid-1980s. One morning while I was busy at my desk with worship bulletin preparation, I looked up to see a beautiful Mein woman with a sleeping baby wrapped snugly on her belly peek her head around the doorway and then look quickly downward. "Come in," I said, standing, and pulling a chair back to indicate that she was welcome. She wrapped one arm around the infant and placed her hand on the back of his curly black head to cradle him while she bent low to honor me, and sat down. She asked me, "What is a Christian?"

All of my years of seminary, all of my training in Aristotle, Gerhard von Rad, and Hans Küng were useless at that moment. For the most part, I had studied the theology of European white males. Latin American and feminist theologians began influencing traditional theology in the seventies and eighties, but these

47

strides in rethinking Eurocentric patriarchal theology had barely influenced the corpus of my seminary education. Christian tradition has long been woefully ignorant of the varieties of religious belief and practice around the globe. Hearing her, I felt embarrassed that I had so little experience of the world from which to respond to her question.

How could I explain *my* Christianity to a woman from Northern Laos? I said a few things about Jesus and told her that I follow his words and teachings. Not knowing her language, I hoped that my emotional fervor aided our communication. "I want to become a Christian," she said. We both grinned broadly and agreed to meet again soon.

Weeks later I learned that her enthusiasm for Christianity had little to do with our conversation that day. When her family was exiled in Northern Laos and running for their lives from the violence of Vietcong soldiers, Christian households opened their homes to sick elderly and gravely wounded refugees. Many people in the region believed that a host family would be spiritually harmed if a stranger died in their home, so the sick and dying were often turned away. But Christian families in the region practiced culture-defying hospitality. These acts of charity had puzzled and impressed her.

Her arrival at my office and the growing presence of Hmong laity and clergy in our area launched the congregation I served into a five-year process of engagement in cross-cultural ministry that required us to acknowledge how little we understand or see beyond the blinders of our own culture. Finding ourselves quite rapidly in a culturally diverse congregation, we had to open our hearts to the stories of others and set aside preconceived notions whenever possible.

The openness of mind to engage in cross-cultural work requires a grace perspective. When we encounter interpersonal differences, our tendency is to fall into comparison, labeling, and establishing hierarchies. When values and traditions appear to be threatened by new or opposing values and traditions, it's easy to lock onto one's own position as the one *true* and *right* position to hold. This is when a shame perspective emerges. We are quick to judge what we do not know, and we even more quickly judge that which we fear. Laying aside all preconceived notions of superiority and inferiority, taking up the perspective of learners among learners, our congregation began to model a welcome to new immigrant families that influenced our larger community. As we proclaimed our equality as children of God, we offered our neighbors an alternative to racist, stigmatizing, and shaming attitudes and behaviors.

Over the next five years, Southeast Asian pastors and laity taught me a deep faithfulness to God that they had forged out of tragedy—fleeing their homelands, fighting a war they did not create, and enduring horrific losses. We became friends and partners in resisting injustice and prejudice in our community, where acts of hostility toward new immigrants occurred weekly. We found common ground in our shared love of children, moments of laughter, and mutual fascination with the Bible and its implications for our lives.

We brought the Hmong and Mein women together (culturally, they are quite different) with the Caucasian women from the congregation to talk about ways to learn from each other. Out of those conversations, a plan was formed to begin classes in sewing and cooking. The Hmong women wanted to know how to cook French fries, donuts, and birthday cakes. The Caucasian women wanted to know how to stuff chicken wings with glass noodles and how to make the delicate curries they had enjoyed at potlucks. The Caucasian women brought their sewing machines to the church and helped the Hmong women interpret the symbols on American patterns. The Hmong women taught classes in the fine stitchery of their story quilts. We set the stage for the community at large to understand and appreciate our differences.

We also had our rough moments. The worship committee was approached by several members of the congregation with complaints that some of our new members were taking off their shoes in the foyer and putting their feet up on the pews during worship. "What should we do?" they asked me in their monthly meeting.

"Tell them they can't do that," one of the committee members remarked. Moses was once advised to take off his shoes, I recalled. "Let's all take off our shoes," I told the surprised committee. "Our sanctuary *is* holy ground." They softened their approach, and some of them thereafter left their shoes in the narthex in solidarity with our new visitors.

Oscar Hammerstein II, in the lyrics he wrote for the musical *South Pacific*, poignantly reminded a nation at war that all of us have been "carefully taught" to fear what is different. Because we have learned to define ourselves as one up or one down on the basis of ethnicity, language, tradition, and behavior, we are likely to reject what we don't understand. In defining our differences, we express and experience shame. "You are not like me." "Shame on you!" This is what was happening when the committee asked me to tell our new members about the unspoken shoe rule. They were subtly expressing a "shame on you" attitude that I carefully noted and addressed. I didn't go to the Southeast Asian community to tell them they were "wrong" for this behavior, as the worship committee may have hoped. Instead, I suggested that if everyone joined in the behavior it would become a new "right" behavior for the whole congregation. We moved from shame to grace.

It's not easy to think and act outside our own cultural constructs. A friend of mine reported an experience at a national church workshop on diversity. Attendees included bishops, laity, judicatory clergy, congregational staff, and employees of several cooperating denominations. For the first two days of the gathering, participants were known by first name only, without any indications of their roles or titles. They became very anxious during those two days, because they were so used to shaping their conversations based on the status and power of the person with whom they were speaking. Without titles or roles to go by, their presumptions were often constructed by gender and racial bias. When at last their identifications became clear, my friend confessed that she had placed people into categories that were blatantly wrong.

Interdenominational clergy and lay leaders at that weekend retreat learned that finding respect and mutuality in diversity depended on more than a desire to do it well; it also required them to confront their previously unexplored cultural biases. After recognizing her own culturally driven thoughts, feelings, and expectations, my friend threw up her hands and said, "The more I know, the more I know I don't know." Like her, we all bump into layers of unexpected shame when we explore diversity. Shame can show up in embarrassment about our ignorance and in attitudes and presumptions about others. Afraid that we might offend someone (shame avoidance), we too often shut down our emotions and stop communicating, thereby missing opportunities for insight, connection, and growing respect.

WHY EXPLORE SHAME AND CULTURE?

A culture is a system of behavioral patterns established by a group of people to ensure right living, the maintenance of order, and the survival of the community. The culture has within it shared values, beliefs, norms, and rituals. Our cultures are the source of rules and taboos. Rules spell out expected behaviors and may be either implicit or explicit. Taboos warn participants that some behaviors will result in punishment or banishment from the group.

Cultural differences in congregations include generations, races, ethnicities, social status, and theology. Consider how difficult it is to satisfy the musical interests of congregations when members span nearly one hundred years of musical history and musical genres from places all over the world. I like a good bluegrass gospel song, because I hail from bluegrass territory. My friend from Texas who grew up near the border of Mexico finds his church music of choice has the flare of mariachi. My friend from New England requires nothing less than an organ solo at full volume when she is worshiping God. Clergy and lay leaders who have not consciously considered the cultural diversity within their congregations contribute to people's ingrained belief that difference is threatening rather than enlivening.

Let's take a closer look at the subject of culture. In a suburban congregation a group of adults came to worship on Sunday escorted by a van driver and woman on the staff of a nearby group home. During worship the differently abled young adults wandered around the sanctuary, sometimes responded to rhetorical questions during the sermon, and chatted with each other during the reading of the Gospel. This behavior caused complaints, and the pastor was presented with a mandate to "go talk to them about the rules." The pastor, recognizing the shame dynamic afoot, asked, "What are the rules?" before going to speak to them. When that question was given to the worship committee, a lively discussion ensued, and they decided to distribute a survey during the worship service. They asked the congregation to fill in check boxes on the survey, indicating which behaviors were okay and which were not okay in worship. The list included things like making noise, ripping a check out of the checkbook, kissing a spouse or partner, raising your hands to ask questions, and walking to the restroom. It identified more than twenty behaviors and included a good deal of humor. The congregation loved it and provided the necessary feedback. It gave them a chance to discuss the value they place on silence during the reading of Scripture and preaching moments. It also put them more at ease when people walked in and out or talked at other times. Once the "rules" were clearer, they revealed what really mattered in worship and what didn't. This made the conversation with the group-home participants lively and educational rather than shaming.

Shame is often the first tool grabbed off the workbench by those entrusted to maintain the status quo. When shame is the primary way of keeping individuals in line with the norms of the community, we are looking at a shame-bound system. This, I believe, is the state of many congregations.

The history of the study of shame and culture has been fraught with difficulty. Over the course of the twentieth century, sociologists, ethnographers, and anthropologists began looking at the subject of shame within cultures. Ruth Benedict (1946)[1] and Margaret Mead (1928)[2] were among the first researchers in the field of anthropology to propose that there are *shame cultures* or *shame societies*. Asian cultures were labeled as such for years, partially due to a lack of understanding of collectivist cultures. Benedict's focus on Japanese society arose just after the close of World War II and in the midst of prejudicial mythologies that had been fostered during the war. Her conclusions that Asian cultures are shame cultures added a stereotype about Asians that increased racism. Shame as a means of family and societal control was thought to be absent in more evolved societies, which scholars now know is not the case. But this stereotype set in place in the mid- to late forties has not been fully eradicated.

Increasing globalization has challenged scholars to explore the universality of the use of shame, but old ideas die hard. Psychologists Gerhart Piers and Milton B. Singer characterized collectivistic cultures as shame cultures as late as 1971.[3] Later studies contradicted their work, however. Harald G. Wallbott and Klaus Scherer in 1995 showed that shame "was experienced with relatively shorter duration, as less immoral, and more often accompanied by laughter and smiles in collectivistic cultures than in individualistic cultures."[4] These later studies suggest that collectivist cultures experience shame differently from individualistic cultures and are not as burdened by it as has formerly been presumed.

Because early studies of shame were steeped in racial and cultural stereotyping, scholars tried another approach, highlighting differences between shame and guilt. More recent scholarship has suggested that Eurocentric or Western cultures are *guilt cultures* or *guilt societies* instead of *shame societies*.[5] This change in terminology appears to be an attempt by Western and Eurocentric scholars to say, "We're different," but still implying "we're better than" cultures of shame. This approach also allowed those researchers to continue in their beliefs that their own cultures had superior values, norms, and taboos and more sophisticated ways to handle errant behaviors. To say that any culture is a shame culture or a shame society (with the implication that *we're not*) shames that culture. I can't say this strongly enough: all cultures use and misuse shame.

How can we even study shame without heaping shame on those who have it? It cannot help us if we apply the concept of shame categorically. Understanding cultural and congregational shame is most helpful when it takes us more deeply into questions of when, how, and why shame is operative within our congregations and in our communities. What does the shame attempt to protect? Does the shame alienate outsiders in order to protect the integrity of a dominant culture? Does shame keep the cultural values intact for future generations? Does it protect members of the group from behaviors that could harm them? These are the questions that clergy and lay leaders need to ask as they engage in changing congregational cultures.

SHAME AND CULTURAL STIGMA

We'd like to think that congregations are more evolved cultures and therefore use less shame than the dominant culture. All cultures, however, use shame to maintain prevailing societal norms by placing stigma on those who appear to be different. After a party at his fraternity, a young man was walking home across campus in the dark. Two male students who saw him thought he was gay. They pulled over to the side of the road and offered him a ride, whereupon they harassed and assaulted him. Gay, lesbian, transgendered, and bisexual youth and adults are often targets of hate crimes. They also endure humiliating shame in the form of social isolation, verbal abuse, or ridicule in front of peers. Shame around sexual orientation appears as frequently within many congregations as it does in the broader culture.

Bullying behavior is another common expression of shame. Teenagers on Facebook and other social media networks have had the freedom to take harassment into the public arena in new ways. While a college student was having sex in his dorm, his roommate secretly videotaped the activity and sent it out live on a social network. Having his private life exposed in this way led to the violated student's suicide. A good deal of conversation is taking place about bullying, but rarely are people naming the underlying emotional content of the bullying, which is shame. What we hate within ourselves becomes the hatred we project onto others. Researchers have found that the majority of those who commit hate crimes were themselves threatened verbally as children or teens. These threats often occur in religious families where sexual diversity continues to be highly feared and stigmatized.

Social control is maintained through shame by those in power. Pastors, Bible study group leaders, youth leaders, sports coaches, and religious educators use shame to keep cohesion and discipline in their groups. I used it myself in a classroom when I was a beginning teacher. Three freshmen girls sat in the back of a class on personality that I was teaching. They giggled and disrupted the class almost every week. A colleague I consulted said flippantly, "Seize control of that class." Next time the class met, I was ready to separate them like grade-school children so that the disruption wouldn't continue. When they started telling private jokes, I walked toward them and said, "Your fellow students deserve to participate without your distracting behaviors." I asked one of them to move to a seat on the other side of the room, and I placed the third one up front near my lectern. The one closest to me made it impossible for me to teach by distracting me with her loud sighs and facial contortions. The next day all three of them marched into the office of the dean to complain about my having "singled them out" in the classroom. When I got a hearing with the dean, it became clear to me that their reaction was directly linked to the fact that I had used shame to publically humiliate them. The fact that I upbraided them in front of their peers made them really angry, which didn't improve the overall sense of well-being in the classroom for me or others. I had to go back to the drawing board and learn to address situations such as this with less shame and greater aplomb.

From then on, I asked students who were acting out to meet me privately in my office prior to the next class session. In one

such meeting, a student who had been falling asleep in class confessed to me that he had an alcohol and drug problem, and I realized that his distracted and distracting classroom behavior was a
cry for help. Had I singled him out with shame, he would not have
offered this confession or gotten the help he needed. Offering
him grace gave him enough dignity to make a change.

Pastors and leaders can be on the alert for similar dynamics
during congregational activities. Since the use of shame can escalate rapidly, leaders need to monitor the use of shame even when
it seems to be only a small element in the organizational system.
With repeated punishment by shame, a shame-bound system of
interactions emerges. Groups can become used to the experience
of shame and learn to use it for discipline and to reinforce norms.
Once established, these shame-bound habits are passed from one
generation to the next.

Shame-bound Congregational Systems

While there are some universal features in the use of shame in
social contexts, congregations vary in the targets they choose to
shame and in their methods of shame reinforcement. As clergy
and congregational leaders, we need to understand the complexity of our use of shame and its use by others in our congregational
systems.

Limited study has been done about the use of shame within congregations of faith, either in the United States or abroad.
Understanding that faith traditions are cultures unto themselves,
however, we can ask pertinent questions about the use of shame
within them. My earlier book, *Sexual Shame: An Urgent Call to
Healing*, lists characteristics of shame-bound congregations that
can be identified. These include communication that is focused
on mistakes and problems rather than strengths and possibilities;
issues couched in "right" and "wrong" terms; "no talk rules" about
secrets and abuses; and an external presentation of greatness that
doesn't match the reality that people experience once they are in

congregational relationships.[6] Congregations that repeatedly use shame develop fixed patterns across generations. My goal is not to shame them for having shame but rather to look into the culture of congregations to find the shame and reduce it.

A Treasurer's Shame Transference

An established pattern of shame may show itself in unexpected ways. In a Midwest congregation, the treasurer of the church was a retired accountant. She knew numbers and figures. Her interpersonal skills were not as well honed. She thought her job was to control every dollar that was raised as well as spent in order to keep the congregation afloat. She became more powerful than the pastor, who did not know what people gave to the congregation. When the budget became tight, she would shame people for turning in receipts. To the Sunday school director she'd say, "Why didn't you buy those supplies yourself?" And to the people who prepared coffee hour she'd say, "I don't think we can afford store-bought cookies. Why don't you make them yourself?" She shamed the pastor too. When he turned in his mileage statement, she would ask him where he had gone and what he had done to "rack up all these miles!" The operational style of the entire system became one of scarcity and shame. Leaders stopped planning programs because they didn't want to have to encounter her in order to get money for their activities, even if they had been voted into a budget. New members learned quickly not to volunteer for simple tasks that involved spending and receipts. Her shame-based criticisms had, in effect, stopped the ministry of the congregation. Everyone felt powerless to stop her. The pastor threw up his hands and asked for reassignment.

When the new pastor arrived, three key leaders decided they had had enough and asked for a consultant to come and help the congregation get back on track. Once the consultant had helped them identify the shame dynamic within their communication patterns, they established communication guidelines for the entire parish. They laid out ways to talk to one another that were appreciative, kind, and supportive. With clearly set norms for the culture of the congregation, leaders agreed to challenge people with love when they were acting from an old pattern of shame or blame. Then they approached the treasurer and asked her to change her behavior or resign. Amazingly, they did this with the same loving acceptance and firm expectations they had agreed to use with the rest of the parish. She changed her behavior, expressed her fatigue from years of "holding the church together," and chose to resign.

Congregations can also develop a shame-bound culture following incidents of clergy or laity sexual harassment or abuse. After misconduct has taken place, most congregations work through issues of guilt and forgiveness, but fewer grapple with lingering shame. Perpetrators have shame about their behavior, though it is deeply hidden under masks of denial and narcissism. Perpetrators may claim to be victims of those they abuse, those who catch them, or those who file charges against them, including judicatory staff, bishops, or the whole congregation. When they deny responsibility for their actions, others pick up and carry the shame. Whole congregations end up with the humiliating shame that these perpetrators have disowned.

The perpetrator's disowned shame is also taken on by their victims. This shame is increased when victims are silenced by congregations, judicatory leaders, or legal settlements involving financial compensation in exchange for a victim's silence or a perpetrator's resignation. When a victim's trust is violated, that person also learns to distrust him- or herself. Harassment and abuse lead victims to conclude that they are totally unworthy of love and communion with God. While victims often leave their congregations in order to be rid of the silence and shame, many of these individuals remain active in worship and congregational leadership long after they are abused. Their silent secrets add to the congregation's level of palpable, albeit unexplained or unexamined, shame. Many clergy have themselves been victims of harassment and abuse, and if they have not been healed of the lingering shame, they unconsciously recreate shame-bound cultures in the congregations where they serve. Shame-bound pastors and congregations often find each other—just as individuals do—and their reluctance to deal with shame makes it hard to identify the roots of a congregation's shame.

THE LEGACY OF CLERGY ABUSE

A man I will call Scott was his pastor's favorite teen in youth group. He was creative and innocent at the age when his spiritual and sexual romanticism flourished. Scott was given the opportunity to meet with the pastor to design programs and retreats for the youth group. He was admired by his pastor for his bright mind and leadership skills and was regularly praised. The pastor became a trusted man in his life, and the congregation became a refuge for Scott. Meanwhile at home his father was withdrawn and absent. His mother and father frequently fought over his father's drinking and late night visits to the local bar. The church was a safer place to hang out, or so he thought. He met more and more frequently with his pastor, who groomed Scott to trust him in everything, shared his personal and sexual thoughts with Scott, and decided to educate Scott about sexuality and how his body worked. The incidents were pleasurable and horrible all at the same time.

It took Scott many years to step inside a counseling office and begin to sort that out. Meanwhile he had been carrying the primary emotion of shame. It invaded his work life, kept him from pursuing a desired career, limited his relationship with his wife, and affected his ability to be close to anyone else, including his own children. The lingering feeling he lived with was "unworthy, unworthy, unworthy," which he tried to compensate for with overwork, codependency, and service to God through work in his local church. He carried a personal legacy of shame, but it also spread among the people with whom he lived and worked.

When leaders of the congregation where his abuse took place were told of these incidents, they were surprised to learn the impact this secret had had on their ministry. They were forced to look at the lingering shame that the congregation had been carrying for years. How could they have shame, you are asking at this moment, if they didn't even know what had happened? This is the insidious nature of shame. It can be found in the unconscious dynamics of the relationships in the congregation. The congregation can develop a shame-bound culture without specific knowledge of incidents that may have created it.

Just like the children in a family where there is a shame-based problem (alcoholism, an affair, a gambling problem), the people in a church family system sense something is amiss, even without knowing it. New visitors have a palpable experience that "something is wrong here." And those closest to the abuse feel the effects of it most acutely. Newcomers to a congregation with abuse shame may notice that everyone just relates to one another on the surface and believe they cannot speak truthfully within the congregational system. New people in a system with a shame-based secret can't find their way into positions of power. Certain subjects aren't talked about (particularly sexual subjects) for fear that well-kept secrets will be revealed. When patterns of shame and secrecy develop, they become habitual within the organizational culture.

You will not find new, healthy leaders staying very long in congregations that have undisclosed secrets. Leaders accustomed to old secrets will likely go on keeping them, and keep new ones as well. Secrets undermine the health and vitality of congregations, because those secrets are surrounded by the emotion of shame. To avoid bumping into shame, systems devise ways to manage and control information surrounding a secret. Congregational secrets are shame-avoidance strategies. They do not address, heal, or eliminate the shame. They contribute to the emotional gridlock of a shame-bound congregation.

When I visit congregations with histories of sexual abuse, embezzlement, and pastors who have had affairs, I am amazed to find that they have hallways (like many congregations) with prominently displayed portraits of their former and current pastors. Some of these clergy have been the ones who have committed gross acts of misconduct and abuse. This gallery of their honored leaders indicates the level to which members deny the problems in their past. While these are meant to be halls of fame, for those who know the history they are in effect halls of shame. If you ask for the portraits to be removed, you will discover the power of the defensive structures that keep members in denial and their shame just under the surface. Ask for stories about those individuals and you may, after much trust has been built, find the truth that could set the congregation free.

You won't likely find the victims of those "hall of shame" clergy in the pews of those congregations on any given Sunday. When victims grow beyond their own shame, they learn to identify shame-bound systems and organizations. They withdraw from unhealthy systems in order to find safety and healing. Unfortunately, their voices are too often silent or missing. These are the people who can provide necessary feedback in order for the system to change.

There are many reasons people who have been raised in congregations do not now worship in them, but too many of them have been deeply wounded by an experience of shame at church. They stay away because they expect to experience shame rather than grace there. They expect to be lectured to, scolded, and admonished, "You should be ashamed of yourself." Many young people see the organizational church as a culture of shame.

WHEN SHAME IS ANTICIPATED

I am neither a sociologist nor a researcher into congregational trends or statistics. What I do know, however, is that over the past few decades, mainline denominations—including Protestant, Catholic, and Jewish congregations in the United States—have been facing a slow and steady decline in membership. Once honored in society as pillars of community virtue, our congregations are now seen as organizations of hypocrisy and irrelevance.

I believe congregations are in decline because they have become shame-bound. Shame is so debilitating that many of our congregations are now critically ill. Shame blocks our ability to evangelize effectively, embrace diversity, and heal individual members. Pervasive shame limits congregation healing after experiences of ineffective and abusive leadership.

At the university where I teach, I once sat listening to a twenty-two-year-old psychology student I'll call Amanda. Amanda was telling me about her search for a church. "I never felt welcomed in the congregations I visited," she said. She went on to describe her first impressions, which included aging congregants, somber moods, and squinty-eyed stares as she walked in the door. "It's like they were suspicious of me!"

Hoping to still hear something positive in her story, I asked her, "What was it like once you took a seat?" She told me that once the prelude began, she had an increasing sense of being out of place. She opened the order of service, and as she read the announcements, she found that they were in code language. They said, "A luncheon will be hosted by the UMW in the FSH. An adult study class on EPH takes place at the usual time in the FSR. Sign up for an upcoming retreat for the UMYF. On Tuesday the trustees will be meeting in the FSH." The only thing on the list that she understood was a note about the work party on Saturday, because it said, "Bring work gloves, pruning sheers, and rakes."

Amanda said that the hymns reminded her of her grandmother's funeral. The preacher invited everyone to stay after the service to chat and drink coffee but never said where to find the room. At sermon time the preacher said, "May the words of my mouth and the meditation of our hearts be acceptable, O Lord," and she wondered if he sometimes made *unacceptable* comments. Just before communion the preacher said that they were all unworthy to come to the table, but some of the people went forward anyway. Amanda sometimes stood up when she should have been sitting down and vice versa. She didn't know the rules, but she was sure she'd broken some of them.

As Amanda became frustrated, she disconnected from what was going on in worship and sent a text message to a friend. "Where are you?" the friend texted back, and Amanda replied with the embarrassed emoticon, a frowning face with red cheeks that is also the emoticon for *shame*. The experience was entirely uncomfortable.

Amanda's story and her words "They were suspicious of me" have stayed with me. Without knowing it, this congregation was sending out messages of shame. They were suspicious of Amanda because the possibility of taking a fresh look at their worship and fellowship evoked uncomfortable feelings inside them too. Perhaps their worship *had* become rote and boring. Amanda might come along and ask too many questions, learn of a conflict they had not resolved or an incident of sexual misconduct that they were keeping secret. Seeing her painfully reminded older members that their own children and grandchildren had long ago abandoned the institutional church. They felt shame about this and about not being able to meet Amanda's needs by providing her with a group of peers within the congregation. And the shame passed to her and back again to them. This shame tossing is all too often the present-day congregational landscape.

No matter how wonderful our programs are, no matter how many people we have in worship, no matter how far our outreach stretches into the community, shame blocks our ability to grow and thrive. I recall a painting I noticed on the wall of a cathedral in Italy. It shows two robed priests, one who faded into the background and one in the foreground who drew my attention. He had his back to me, but he was looking over his shoulder at me too. He was holding a Bible in the crook of his left arm, and his right hand was raised with his index finger pointing over his shoulder right at me as I looked into the scene. I could almost hear him making that clicking sound, "Tut, tut, tut." Or perhaps he was saying, "Shame on you!" Do you know someone who doesn't come to church because this is what they expect to experience?

As our congregations age and we watch our beloved institutions lose their influence in society around us, the more we experience the shame of failure. Only with a transparent review of our mistakes and secrets, an acceptance of our own congregational climates, and clearly defined goals can we create something new and lively again. Good people make bad decisions. It is perilous to bolster congregational esteem by self-righteous condemnation of others. We need to be open to change and to being challenged to change when "the other" arrives in our midst.

Jesus's Progression from Shame to Grace

The fear of "the other" is a sign of the depth of shame in congregational attitudes and behaviors. Jesus was part of a culture that also used shame to distinguish the righteous from the unrighteous.[7] He engaged in dialogue on many occasions with those whom others had shamed. His approach to the tax collector, the leper, and the woman of Samaria showed his openness to growing beyond shame and to replacing judgment with grace. In a short story in Mark 7:24–30, we read about Jesus's encounter with one woman in particular. He goes into a house for a bit of rest and a good hot meal, but the story says Jesus "did not want anyone to know that he was there. Yet he could not escape notice, but a woman whose little daughter had an unclean spirit immediately heard about him, and she came and bowed down at his feet . . . and begged him to cast the demon out." The woman was an outsider, "a Gentile, of Syrophoenician origin." Jesus's response has surprised and puzzled interpreters for decades. He appears to dismiss her when he refers to her as a "dog" to whom one wouldn't throw the children's food. He sees her as an outsider and shames her. With courage she answers him, saying that even the dogs under the table eat the crumbs that fall. We wonder what he was thinking in the pause between his comments and her response. Was he willing to correct his insider-outsider approach? Was he willing to be shameless in his subsequent responses? Indeed, he is: "For saying that, you may go—the demon has left your daughter." He reverses his dehumanizing position, and the mother returns home to find that her daughter has been healed.

What can we learn from this story? It takes openness and compassion to reverse shame and a willingness to be taught by "the other." As Jesus has shown us the way, we too can catch ourselves in the act of shaming, and then do the unexpected by offering grace.

CHAPTER 4

The Shame-Blame Game
Recognizing Shame's Opposite

I prepared a workshop for a congregation in which several incidents of sexual abuse had occurred. The new pastor, eager to heal old wounds, invited me to come, but when the time for the event drew near lay leaders resisted. They said, "Please don't come and blame us for what has happened here." Why would they expect blame? In systems dynamics, blame is the projection of unwanted shame. Draw a line on a sheet of paper and put shame at one end and blame at the other. They are on the same emotional line. Because shame feels so terrible, we avoid it through the use of blame. For example, a husband gets home after work, having forgotten his wife's request to pick up milk at the store. He doesn't feel good about it, may even feel shame he can't admit to, so he comes in the door with a defensive strategy—blame the wife for not writing him a note so he'd remember. Or, a church secretary omits a section of the newsletter that a lay leader handed to her a few months ago. She doesn't like feeling that she let the leader down, so she defends herself against this emotion by mounting a long defense about her lack of time in the front office with too many demands from the pastor to do other tasks. This is the reason, she asserts without apology, that the article was overlooked.

When you begin to look for shame in a congregation, it may be easier to spot in the inverse emotion of blame.

Another way blame shows up is that when people feel a good deal of shame about something, they convict themselves and expect others to join them in it. Here's how the pattern worked in the congregation mentioned above that suffered from multiple abuses, secrets, and residual wounds. What the lay leaders felt was shame, but it was expressed in their expectation that they would be blamed for all that had happened. As we talked about the incidents, I learned that leaders felt as if they were somehow responsible for injuries that had resulted from staff boundary crossings. They didn't know exactly *what* they had been doing that contributed, but they expected to be chastised for it. They had experienced this dynamic before. Unwilling to acknowledge his own shame, a staff member who had been let go several years ago spent months telling everyone in the community that he was mistreated by the personnel committee. Perpetrators of abuse are unlikely to take responsibility for their actions, and they commonly blame the lay leaders and the congregation for their professional misconduct.

To lower the shame in a congregation like this, I had to start by reducing blame. I reassured them that I wasn't coming to blame them and that I had great compassion for the pain they continued to experience from secrets and abuse. I knew that with reduced shame, they could eventually acknowledge the systems dynamics that had contributed to the abuse pattern. This congregation learned to end abuse and learned ways to end the shame-blame dynamic that came along with it.

Following incidents of clergy sexual abuse, it's common to hear comments such as, "Why didn't we have policies in place?" "Why didn't we stop it?" and "Why didn't we see it coming?" "We should have known!" is the exacerbated cry of those who missed signs of abuse or observed things they brushed away, denied, or ignored. The voice of shame has a lot of *should* and *should haves* within it. Blame points an index finger around a room until it finds a target, insisting someone else is the guilty party.

The shame-blame dynamic appears in congregations without histories of abuse too. When Alice became the new pastor at Centennial Congregation, she felt confident and ready for her ministry. She was at a midpoint in her career and prepared to take on a larger congregation with a mission of service in the community. She made relationships quickly and established trust early in her tenure. While the office wing of the church building was being renovated, she was often on-site working in the vicinity of the contractors, but she handled their questions by directing them to Martin, the building committee chairperson. Prior to his retirement, Martin had worked for years in contracting, and he liked his congregational role as supervisor of the project. When decisions about the project were made, or emergencies arose, he told Alice "not to worry your pretty little head about it" and to call him right away.

On Saturday afternoon when Alice arrived to get some books out of her office to finish her sermon, she found a leak that was quickly spreading behind the bathroom wall. She called Martin but he didn't answer his cell phone. She left him a message about the emergency and called him again an hour later. At that point she called the contractor directly, authorized him to call the plumbing contractor, and agreed that the congregation would pay for the weekend rate to get the problem solved. The repair was made late in the day, and at about 5:00 p.m. she got a call from Martin who was home after an afternoon excursion and ready to "get down there and fix it." She told him that she'd called the contractor and that the repair had been made. But Martin was not thankful. He was furious! He began to berate her on the phone about spending money the church "doesn't have" and told her she did not have the authority to approve the repair. "Your job is to preach and visit people at the hospital," he yelled. "My job is to handle the building project." He finished his tirade, "You'd better mind your place, little lady!" and hung up the phone.

Alice was shaken and angry at that point, but having been raised in a culture of politeness and having learned to put up with gender harassment and verbal abuse, she put on a good face the next morning at church. Martin gathered a group of male peers in the corner of the social hall after the service to rage about what had happened to him, acting like a victim in this situation. What Martin felt underneath his anger was shame for having not responded sooner and not handled the problem himself. He thought he had let the congregation down by not being on the job 24/7 like he told them he would be. He was embarrassed about having left his cell phone at home that afternoon and having never received the calls from Alice. But these were feelings of vulnerability, and he wasn't at all comfortable with them. In Martin's mind, one mistake was a grave flaw in his character that he didn't want to admit to anyone, including his cronies on Sunday morning. His unconscious emotional strategy was to get the shame off himself by placing blame on Alice. If he could make the cost overrides her fault, he wouldn't have to admit that he had, in his own self-critical mind, failed to do his job.

Additionally, an insidious gender-based shame-blame pattern arose. He set the stage with his peers by describing Alice as "too controlling," a label often applied to women who have authority and use it. In his mind she was impatient, had overreacted, and had usurped his proper authority. He undermined her power and authority, which allowed him to keep a safe psychological distance from his shame. Alice had limited options for changing the dynamic with Martin but quickly tired of trying to figure him out. Rather than join the blame and shame game, she took the entire situation to the personnel committee for discussion and feedback. This empowered them to work together with Martin to honor the work he was doing, which lowered his defensiveness. Then they let him know how unhelpful his blaming was and asked him to stop it.

SHAME OVERLAYS CONGREGATIONAL GRIEF

When congregations fall into decline, they are even more likely to develop patterns of blame and shame. Rather than experience the grief of having lost generations of new members, the pain of ineffectiveness in keeping the ministry growing and vital in their communities, or the despair of a congregation likely to close in the next decade, they turn on each other like piranha in a small fish tank. In a congregational meeting on evangelism, for example, congregants talk about why their membership is declining: "I think that we've never recovered from the bishop yanking Stan away right in the midst of our seven-year plan to revitalize!" "I know Stan didn't want to go; he told us so." "Yeah, I think we'd have turned the corner if Stan had stayed on." "Maybe, but I think that young people just don't want to be part of groups like this anymore." "They are too busy watching football, going to youth soccer games, and catching up on chores to come here on Sunday mornings." "I think the pastor isn't doing enough to reach out to them." "I think we haven't been growing because the elders in this congregation never want to let go of the reins." "We have to keep our big donors happy to keep the bills paid, right?" Notice that in each of the statements, someone is being blamed.

These congregational leaders had been ineffective for fifteen years, ever since Stan secretly approached his bishop about wanting to change churches. Curiously, when Stan left, they abandoned the plan they had begun under his leadership rather than sticking with it on their own. They had clearly been disempowered, even during Stan's tenure, perhaps expecting him to be the miracle maker. Stan added to their disempowerment by never confessing to congregational leaders that he himself had approached the bishop about a move to a "better" congregation. Stan told them his move was the bishop's fault so that he could avoid his own shame for abandoning them in the midst of their work together and so they wouldn't blame him. They blamed the bishop for leaving them victimized and bereft. It was easier to do that than to take up the task of finishing their formerly good plan for revitalization.

We also see that the congregation blamed the young people of the community for their lack of interest and availability. Rather than take ownership of the situation and come up with new outreach strategies, they were stuck in the shame-blame dynamic.

They could have offered services at alternative times, for example, or asked the families in their neighborhood what they might need from the congregation. Instead, they were defensive about their lack of young people and blamed the whole recalcitrant genera- tion. In the last few comments they make, we see these leaders blaming the congregation itself. The elders are to blame for being stodgy and unwilling to change with the times.

In some situations, pastors join the shame-blame dynamic by labeling the congregation resistant, unwilling to change, or stuck in their ways. Clergy can push away their own feelings of being ineffective leaders by saying that their congregations aren't open to new ideas. The pastor says, "We'd grow if it weren't for those oldsters," and the matriarchs and patriarchs say, "We'd grow if our pastor would just _____." You can fill in the blank with a vari- ety of expectations, all of which boil down to blame. When we can blame someone else for a problem, we avoid taking responsibil- ity for any part in it. We say instead, "It's the bishop," "It's those people who don't want to join us," "It's the pastor," or "It's the oldsters." *They* are the problem.

Shame is such an uncomfortable and disempowering emotion that blame seems a better option. Blame is a powerful and self- protective emotion. In the way that anger is recruited as an emo- tional substitute for sadness, people recruit blame as an emotional substitute for shame. People feel stronger when they are blaming. They feel self-righteous. Blame protects them from vulnerability and weakness, which are experienced along with shame. It's a more attractive option than shame.

This process of shame and blame leaves everyone feeling sul- lied and unclean. In situations where people are getting hurt, what is the Christian ethic? Should you take the blame, and take it again, or stand up in defiance and refuse it? In Luke's Gospel Jesus sets out an ethic for loving one's enemies by doing good to those who hate you, blessing those who curse you, and praying for those who abuse you (Luke 6:27–28). This may appear to be an ethic of passivity in the face of injustice and violence. Is he suggesting that we take the blame? In the next verse the hearer is really thrown off base by Jesus saying, "If anyone strikes you on the cheek, offer the other also." This ancient text describes the way that shame and blame can be transferred from one person to another in the form of violence.

In the cultural world of Jesus and his followers, a blow to the cheek would have most likely been by a right hand to the left cheek of the opponent. The slap was an attempt by the assailant to humiliate (shame) the opponent. Once the assailant had injured you with the right hand, turning the right cheek forward would have challenged the assailant to use the left hand for further blows. But in Jesus's society, the left hand wasn't used in public. It was considered unclean, because it was used for unclean tasks, such as personal hygiene. In the court of law, a gesture with the left hand was punishable by ten days of penance. In the language of shame, the first blow would have placed shame on the cheek of the victim. When the victim presented the other cheek, the perpetrator could not strike again without being shamed too.

According to biblical theologian Bob Funk, this cheek-turning mandate is about power and strength rather than passivity and victimization. Funk notes, "To turn the other cheek under the circumstance was an act of defiance." Turning the other cheek forced the assailant to do something awful, to use the left hand against the opponent's cheek. This would have brought great shame to the one delivering the left-handed second strike, so at this point, the assault would most likely have ended. Funk concludes, "The humiliation of the initial blow was answered with a nonviolent, very subtle, but quite effective challenge. The act of defiance entailed risk; it was symbolic, to be sure, but for that reason appealed to those who were regarded as subservient inferiors in Jesus's world."[1] This small story freed Jesus's audience from any obligation to participate in shameful humiliation.

As I try to understand Jesus's message in its original context, I find a message about the strength of moral force we acquire when we refuse to be shamed and the challenge that those who try to shame us will be shamed as well. This is a liberating message for women who have too often been counseled by their pastors to "turn the other cheek" when they are abused by their spouses. The story ironically implies the opposite, that we can stop ongoing shame and abuse by resisting it. In Jesus's teaching about turning the other cheek, the attempt to blame and humiliate is met with a strong stand, the turn of the head, the look that says, "I refuse to take on the shame of your aggression," and if you do that again, the shame will fall back upon you in even greater portion.

Pastoral theologian Robert H. Albers, in his book *Shame: A Faith Perspective,* calls blame "the scapegoating defense." He says that in this dynamic "Neither the blamer nor the one blamed ultimately deals with their sense of shame."[2] Clergy and lay leaders create wellness in their congregations when they identify patterns of blame and courageously look at the unhealed shame beneath them. How can we get underneath the blame to encourage others to own and explore even more painful emotions?

SKILLS TO USE FOR SHAME REDUCTION

While not all lay leaders and clergy are trained in skilled listening, many do possess the qualities needed to reduce shame. Let's go back to the comments of the evangelism committee and see if a few questions would help the people who are engaging in the shame-blame process to go deeper and to acknowledge their feelings.

Someone in the congregation says, "I think that we've never recovered from the bishop yanking Stan away right in the midst of our seven-year plan to revitalize!" and someone else says, "I know Stan didn't want to go; he told us so." This would be a good time to ask, "What was it like for you when your plans all went awry?" If participants could be redirected to their own thoughts, feelings, and experiences, they would be better able to talk about powerlessness, abandonment, and vulnerability during those times. When others say, "Maybe, but I think that young people just don't want to be part of groups like this anymore," a fellow leader who hears the blame in the statement could ask, "Is there something we could learn from them, rather than being angry or disappointed in them?" When the pastor is blamed, a lay leader could interrupt the pattern by simply saying, "Hey, we're a team with the pastor. What can we do to improve this situation?" With a firm belief that no one is at fault and that congregations go through cycles of birth, vitality, stagnation, productivity, and death, just as people do, a leader can help others move from finding fault to addressing problems with a belief in the capacity of the congregation to right itself, heal itself, transform itself.

I recently heard myself in a session with a client say, "I don't want to be the only person in the room who believes in the possibility that you can have a happy future." This needs to be the position of congregational leaders too. Even if everyone for generations has been stuck in destructive patterns, leaders who have hope in growth-filled change can redirect the focus away from blame and shame. Negativity needs to be named and explored. One thing I have learned as a therapist is that resistance to change is simply information about what needs to take place in preparation for that change. When congregants appear to be stuck in the past, loyal to old ways or former days, they are expressing resistance to change. But underneath their surface comments lies a wealth of information about them. What has hurt them and left them untrusting? What has blocked them from seeing their own potential? What needs to be done to make change possible? Blaming the pastor, the judicatory, fellow congregants, or people who don't come to worship is so destructive that it needs to be named for what it is. A good question to ask in the face of it is, "What does blaming keep us from thinking and feeling about ourselves?"

John Gottman, who has published many books on couples' relationships, describes contempt as one of four key signs that, without immediate intervention, the end of the relationship is inevitable. He defines *contempt* as "statements that come from a relative position of superiority."[3] Because contempt may include cynicism, verbal abuse, sarcasm, name calling, rolling of the eyes, sneering, mockery, and hostile humor, it seems to be a clear parallel to blame. Gottman notes that contempt is the greatest predictor

of divorce. We could also predict that contempt has the power to
end pastoral tenures and destroy congregational relationships.

I had a recent conversation with a colleague about her new
job at a local nonprofit organization. In her new workplace, co-
workers are encouraged to be open with their feelings during staff
meetings. This sounded to her like a healthy idea, but she soon
learned that people interpreted this openness as permission to
lob personal attacks at one another. On mornings when she had
to go to those meetings, she had to skip her usual breakfast due
to anxiety and stomachaches. Her thought was that if co-workers
were willing to blame and shame others, it wouldn't be long before they turned that behavior toward her. A conversation with
her supervisor was fruitless.

Her supervisor was unable to understand or address the shame-
blame dynamic that was destroying co-workers' relationships. A
wiser supervisor would have set ground rules for the group and
taught them to more effectively discuss their experiences with one
another. They would all have been asked to take responsibility
for creating respectful partnerships. To eliminate blame, leaders
need the humility and humor to know that what we hate in others
is likely what we also dislike in ourselves. In any workplace or congregation, leaders need to gently remind constituents that blame
is out-of-bounds behavior and then redirect the conversation to
the deeper feeling of inadequacy or shame that hides beneath it.

The older I get, the bolder I become in confronting some of
these negative behaviors. Early in my career, being liked was more
important to me than speaking up when others were saying hurt-
ful things. I made a key mistake and learned a key lesson in the
first parish I served. After taking a few months of leave to have
a baby, I heard many rumors that people didn't like the student
intern who had filled in for me. The intern was blamed for my
"abandonment" of the parishioners to take care of my own infant.
Eventually they began to also blame me for being out of the office too long and for nursing my infant at the church when they
wanted to find me at coffee hour, and they became jealous and
needy due to the attention I was giving my infant.

So, once I returned to full-time ministry, I decided to tackle these problems in a straightforward way. I phoned everyone who anyone had told me was upset about the situation and offered to come over to their homes to hear their concerns. I went and they unloaded with things like, "We wouldn't have so many juvenile delinquents in the world if it weren't for working mothers," and, "If you wanted to be a mother, why didn't you think that through before becoming our pastor?" Their comments indicated a level of dependency on the pastor that they were not fully aware of and therefore had never discussed.

They also expressed resistance to the idea of having a woman pastor and all that this newness entailed. One man who had been complaining to his friends that "everything had fallen apart" while I was gone was open with me during my visit. As he, his wife, and I sat and drank coffee and ate cookies, she told me that he was still grieving the loss of the former pastor. I asked him to tell me more about that. He became red in the face and said, "The problem with you is that we can't go golfing together, because you don't golf." He had never asked me if I played golf, of course. What he meant was that because I was a woman, he didn't know how to relate to me. This brought up his feelings of disconnection, inadequacy, and shame. I gently thanked him for his openness. Although he was clearly angry with me, he had still trusted me by describing the underlying issues that formed his judgment about my ministry. I was able to understand his grief, and confessed that even if the gender differences had not set up rules for us about acceptable ways for us to relate, I did not, alas, play golf.

Most of the parishioners I visited were not as candid. In the end, I learned that I didn't need to go chasing after the negativity of parishioners. When they made me a target, I asked other members to tell them to stop it. When blame was running amok, I trained leaders to challenge it and to assist one another in getting to underlying feelings. We all agreed to refrain from blame and to take shared responsibility for our thoughts, our actions, and our congregation.

At gatherings of clergy, I listen to the table talk of my colleagues. Many of them are tired, frustrated, and suffering from what psychologists call professional burnout. This is expressed in shame-blame language. "My congregation just isn't open to new ideas," one of them says; another, "My people expect too much from me." And another says, "I'd never met a meaner bunch of Christians." Underneath these comments lies a whole host of other feelings, including emotional exhaustion, low self-esteem, and ineffectiveness.

When an interim pastor decided that the congregation's three worship services would be reduced to one, he set about convincing the congregation by using the shame-blame game. Those who wanted to retain three services were called divisive and cliquish rather than diverse and unique. Leaders who spoke to him alone found that he didn't have the stamina to conduct all three services and had a very personal agenda for the change. His fatigue was a source of shame for all of them, but they kept quiet about it as they went about changing everything possible about corporate worship. The whole process backfired into name calling, blame, and contempt.

When clergy feel their efforts are thwarted by congregational resistance, they often become less healthy by overworking and cheerleading their congregations. These leaders take up new congregational projects or programs of revitalization. These efforts won't succeed if the underlying emotional climate involves shame for all that has not yet been done or can't be done in the present day or will not be done in the future. If the relational life of the congregation is filled with blame for past injuries, current impotence, or the thwarting of future plans, the congregation will become stagnant. The way out of shame-blame is to explore these negative emotions and patterns and to accept with grace everyone who has fallen into their traps. The relational health of the congregation, of lay leaders and clergy, must become shame-less and blame-less before vitality can be restored.

CHAPTER 5

Comparison Shame
Closing the Gaps with
Acceptance and Respect

Children are inquisitive about difference and remarkably bold. Walking alongside his clergy mother on the way into church one Sunday morning, Joey, who was five at the time, asked the woman walking next to them if she had a penis. His innocent curiosity was met with stony silence, but he could tell that she was shocked by the question. She blushed, turned away from him, and walked at a faster pace. The little boy's mother squeezed his hand firmly and told him, "We don't ask that kind of question in public!" The child became acquainted with shame that morning when his curiosity was met with his mother's frowns and whispers.

During the fellowship hour after worship in another congregation, a towheaded ten-year-old girl walked over to a young African American woman and asked her if her blood was red or brown. The little girl's inquisitiveness was met by a patient and graceful response from the woman she had approached, who smiled at her and said simply, "All blood is red, just the same in all of us." But when the little girl noticed the horrified look on her father's face, her normal curiosity was infused with another feeling. By unintentionally displeasing her father, she lost his "at-a-girl" smile and experienced the discomfort of shame.

Children learn that noticing and pointing out human differences is "wrong." We celebrate their fascination with the uniqueness of each snowflake or variations in tree species but discourage comments about gender, race, religion, or status. Children soon learn that people divide themselves into categories like good, better, and best. As they grow older, healthy curiosity gives way to comparison shame.

The term *comparison shame* describes the emotional weight that accompanies negative comparisons. Individuals in social contexts judge themselves alongside others, and using various classifications, they establish rank or status. We all use categorization to find and secure our place in the world. Like Jesus's disciples jockeying for the best seat at the table or vying for a place at God's right hand for eternity, we can easily end up in the comparison-shame trap.

In this chapter, I will explore comparison shame and ways it sneaks into daily life for individuals, families, and congregations. We begin our lives in an innocent stage and quickly learn to make distinctions between groups of people by gender, appearances, peer relationships, and more. We also learn to distinguish between our family and others, our racial identity and others, our religion and others. Across the lifespan, more and more experiences set the stage for us to experience comparison shame. We develop friendships and form peer groups, date and find lovers and life companions, and join social communities for work, worship, and political action. Each venue provides opportunities to appreciate individual and social diversity—or for comparison shame. Clergy and lay leaders who learned comparison shame while growing up may also find it commonplace in congregational life. Being familiar with functional shame can lead to complacency and the tendency to tolerate it. Leaders can learn instead to identify, name, and end comparison shame.

COMPARISON SHAME IN FAMILY RELATIONSHIPS

My mother entered the freshman hallway at North High School, put her coat in her locker, and went off to class, following in her older brother's footsteps. He was two years ahead of her, received top grades in every class, and was destined to provide the valedictorian speech at commencement. Entering either history or English class—it wouldn't have mattered which one—the teacher noticed her last name. "Oh, are you Bill's sister?" the teacher asked. "Yes," she said, wondering what comment would follow. The teacher extended his hand in a firm handshake and asked, "Are you as smart as he is?" She blushed, shrugged her shoulders, and took a seat toward the back of the room. When teachers compared my mother to her brother, they reinforced my mother's shame that she could never measure up alongside him.

Comparison isn't always a bad thing in and of itself. For example, most colleges and seminaries offer classes in comparative religions. As I discussed in the previous chapter about cross-cultural relationships, comparing for the sake of learning and understanding can increase one's respect for differences. But when comparison is used with an underlying goal of confirming superior or inferior status, shame fills the gaps. With comparison shame we are not just different, we are different better or worse, different smarter or dumber, capable or inept, valid or invalid. We live with all manner of comparative dualisms. The more shame we carry, the more likely we are to divide the world into levels of goodness or wretchedness.

My mother's school experiences recurred. She did not feel humbler because of these comments. She felt humiliated. Eventually she told her teachers, "I am not as smart as my brother is," and she hid out near the back of the room. There are lots of ways to measure intelligence, so we'll never know whether she was as smart as her brother. By the time I heard this story from mother she had learned to keep her "place." Despite earning an advanced degree in library science and achieving excellent grades in college, however, she never fully acknowledged her own brilliance. While she remained too timid to take pride in her accomplishments, she eventually moved beyond the shame.

One of the many maxims she repeated to us children was, "You may be better than some people, and you may be worse than some people, but always remember—you are just as good." Because of mother's experiences growing up in the shadow of her talented brother, she never allowed me to think of myself as superior to anyone. She challenged any self-righteous attitude that cropped up, and the word *stupid* was forbidden in our household. As an adolescent Christian, I started dividing the world into Christians (good) and nonbelievers (bad). One day I mentioned to my mother that my sister's husband was in pitiable shape and would likely go to hell for his unbelief. She sternly looked at me over the top of her reading glasses and said, "Now wait a minute, young lady!" I learned the futility of separating the world into sheep and goats. She wouldn't tolerate shame in our household. Her no-shame approach made me a better person and a better preacher—I can't say I'm better than anyone else, of course, just better than I would have been without her guidance.

Comparisons naturally arise among siblings, members of extended families, and partners. We also compare up and down across generations. We all like to think of ourselves as more evolved (better) than the last generation. Yet many of us are also taught that to be happier, more successful, or wealthier than our parents would be disloyal. As we grow into adulthood, strong family loyalties incline us to set our aspirations no higher than those of our parents. Additionally, we accept an unspoken assumption that we will be as depressed, as anxious, as codependent, or as addicted as our parents, following the family edict that this is required of good children. Resisting this generational pattern, a wise friend once noted, "I refuse to live down to my father's expectations of me." Others of us spend our lives trying to exceed our parents' predictions of how we will turn out. If our parents were extremely successful, the pressure to do as well may also leave us feeling hopelessly unworthy.

Husbands, Wives, Partners, and Lovers

Another form of comparison shame arises when we are compared to our spouses and partners. When I was walking through a grave-yard with a friend, we noticed a beautiful grave marker, a tall stone square with a marble obelisk. On the front it said, "The Honorable Rev. Duncan, 'He loved the Lord and fed His sheep.'" On the back was an epitaph for the wife of the Rev. Duncan that read, "She did what she could." Compared to her husband, she apparently fell a little short of the glory of God. One wonders whether the poor thing ever made it into heaven or went, in shame, straight into hell. Rev. Duncan's wife could not live up to her husband's character and will remain shamed on her epitaph until the marble collapses and returns to dust. Did she live her whole life in comparison to him? Did she agree to the sentence on her side of the monument?

Comparison shame arises for couples when their differences seem to threaten the survival of the relationship. If couples become so close to each other that their identities become merged, they will push away from each other to establish their own uniqueness. They may use comparison shame in this process. If they become anxious that they are losing themselves in the relationship, they will assert their differences by shaming their partners. In response to the fear of merging, they push back from the relationship and declare, "I'm not like *that*! I'm like *this*." Asserting "I'm different from you" is helpful. Insisting "I'm okay and you're not okay" is indicative of comparison shame.

When conflicts escalate between partners, we typically defend ourselves, but a better approach is to define ourselves. For example, after overhearing her spouse's conversation, Mary asks Lenny, "Why don't you tell your mother what you really think?" and Lenny defends the behavior, offering many good reasons for it, all of which Mary dismisses. To move beyond being shamed (for being too timid or weak-kneed with his mother) or shaming back (for making him defend himself), the couple needs to move toward definition rather than defense. Mary could try to learn more about Lenny by suspending her judgment and saying, "I'm curious about the fact that you tell me how you feel, but you don't tell your mother." Her observation prompts Lenny to say, "I suppose you could tell your mother anything (laughing), because sometimes from my view you say amazing things to her. But in our family, we weren't safe speaking up. We'd be inviting Mother's wrath by suggesting anything to her." Mary can now understand more about Lenny's behavior, and even if she would handle the situation differently, she feels more respect for his decisions about what to say to his mother.

This conversation moves the couple from a place of comparison shame to comparison grace, the kind of comparison that says, "We're different aren't we?" and that says, "It's okay that we're different; we can learn from each other." We enter dangerous waters when we move from comparison for the sake of appreciation to comparison that shames. Old messages from childhood emerge as we try to cope with our partner's uniqueness. "If we're not the same, then one of us is wrong." When couples face different levels of desire for time together, affection, or sexual frequency, they can quickly become angry or hurt by their differences.

The Woody Allen film *Annie Hall* uses a split screen to show a married couple, both seeing their therapists, at the same time. His therapist asks, "How often do you sleep together?" and the man laments, "Hardly ever. Maybe three times a week." His wife is asked by her therapist, "Do you have sex often?" and she responds, "Constantly. I'd say three times a week."[1] The humorous inference is that he wants it too much and she wants it too little. In sexuality, where we are especially vulnerable to feelings of shame, our differences require conversations of respect and openness. Humor can also go a long way to help us recognize the dangerous territory of proclaiming, "I'm right, you're wrong."

We are complex and multifaceted people. Most of us spend a lifetime learning to befriend *our own* longings, foibles, and follies and then we face the task of appreciating someone else's. We may need to learn to treat our own ideas and feeling with respect in order to provide that respect to our partners. My husband and I often talk about our more difficult subjects while we take the dog out for a walk. During one particular end-of-the-day walk when we were both a bit tired, he noticed that our voices were getting a little louder as the conversation heated up. Sensing that we were beginning to take entrenched positions, he chuckled and then commented, "I've already lost this fight, so give me time to do my homework and come back to this for round two." We are blessedly different, and to maintain a graceful relationship we carefully avoid shaming each other about heartfelt positions.

In our families and partnerships, with our friends, and in organizational systems we have the opportunity to learn more about ourselves through the mirrors that others hold before us. One of those mirrors, a look of shame on the face of a trusted loved one, can be devastating and can also produce defensive anger. When hurt or anger arises in response, moving from defensiveness to definition takes some practice and humility, but we cannot do it if we feel ashamed. Becoming shame-less allows us to approach comparisons with less emotional attachment to them. Then we can catch shame-laden comparisons when they arise and redirect that energy toward creating contented, joyful, and satisfying relationships.

COMPARISON TO THE PAST AND THE FUTURE

Another comparison trap sets us up for shame. When we compare today's reality with a nostalgic past or an imagined brighter future, we may fail to experience the thoughts, feelings, and pleasures of the current day. If we look back and say, "That was the best time in my life" or "I've never been happier," we end up comparing a happy past to a less happy present. If we put our focus on a life we think we could have had or should have had, shame becomes the dominant emotion. Perhaps we initiated a divorce and we feel a lingering sense of failure about it. Perhaps a loved one died, and we became stuck in the irrational feeling that we could have prevented it. Perhaps we went through a time of sexual exploration that left us with lingering shame. Being older, wiser, or more enlightened in the present day doesn't mean that we should return to former mistakes and shame ourselves for them.[2]

Negative comparisons keep us from delighting in the present. "You used to *like* lima beans," a frustrated parent will say to a teenager, with an underlying tone of anger. A spouse will say to her partner, "We used to go on long trips together," with a wistful sigh for the long lost past. When "used to" enters the conversation, be on the alert for shame. When relationships fall into difficult patterns of regret and blame, shame is the hidden affect. The language of comparison shame arises to mask anger and disappointment. Catching the shame dynamic allows us to look beneath the surface to find our deep and true longings for connection or to admit that the connection has ended.

Recognizing elements of the past that we can grasp or reengage in today might help us feel good about ourselves, but lingering back there sometimes increases shame. For example, a couple may find that their relationship was more satisfying when they had a regular date night or when they took spontaneous weekend trips to the mountains or when they lingered in bed together on a Saturday morning. A conversation about the past may provide them with clues about how to nurture a happy relationship right now. If they throw "You used to . . ." language about the good times into their daily conversations, the relationship will head quickly downhill. Lowering comparison shame involves staying in the present moment, accepting the emotional content of this moment, observing thoughts and feelings, and honoring them. In grace-filled relationships the past is just the past, not better or worse, and the present, even with pain and difficulty, is valued and valuable.

Backward glances may be inaccurate and deceptive. In every era in our lives we encounter a mixed bag of joys, challenges, and growth. Locking our thoughts onto an idealized past leads to disappointment and frustration and locking our thoughts onto an idealized future can leave us ashamed and hopeless about getting there, wherever there *should* be. Preoccupation with any time other than now disrupts peace and acceptance in the present day. Because we can conjure up shame quickly, it is essential when looking backward or forward to avoid the trap of shame-based comparisons. Russ Harris, physician and author, notes the difficulty of avoiding past or future thinking: "The past and future only exist as thoughts occurring in the present. We can plan for the future, but that planning happens here and now. We can reflect on and learn from the past, but that reflection happens in the present. This moment is all we ever have."[3] In this present moment, we can become shame-less by offering full acceptance and grace to ourselves about those past events and by accepting that we are whole, well, and lovely in the present moment.

COMPARISONS BY CLERGY AND CONGREGATIONS

The ways that comparison shame damages individuals, couples, friends, and families occur in congregations too. Clergy and lay leaders experience comparison shame when the present is compared to a nostalgic past or an idealized future, and when they compare their congregation to the one next door that is attracting more new members or building a new building. Lay leaders add shame to the mix when they compare their pastor to a former pastor, some idealized pastor, or even to Jesus. As you read this section, I think you will see the overlapping dynamics of family systems and congregational systems. Whenever two or more are gathered, shame is likely to enter into those relationships.

Ask these questions about your congregation. Is curiosity discouraged? Are people shamed for asking questions, probing into the past, or addressing sexual topics? Is difference met with defensiveness? Are preachers and pivotal lay leaders negatively compared to one another? Is the congregation wistfully longing for the past or shamefully regretful about the past? Is there room in congregational leadership for new ideas, new approaches, and new plans? Are there limits to how happy, successful, and fruitful congregations can become? The relational dynamic of comparison shame limits congregational health and growth, as seen in the following illustrations.

Many of our denominations flourished in the 1940s and '50s, and congregations were hubs of dating, social prestige, and community activity at that time. Parishioners may look back with fondness and wonder about why those days can't simply be recreated. Huge social changes—such as a decrease in the availability of volunteers, shrinking family time in households with working parents, and changes in sexual norms and behaviors across the past three decades have separated congregations from the dominant culture and have left congregations floundering. Still, many congregations hold on to the notion that church "back then" was the way church should be.

The intractable belief that the congregation of more than half a century ago is relevant today goes beyond reasoning. The emotional component underlying this problem is comparison shame. Rather than firmly grasp the reality that we can no longer conduct business as usual and make radical changes in the culture of congregations, the shame we feel about being "less than" we were leaves us stuck and impotent. Participants in congregations bump against it while trying to create new programs, to think beyond the boxes of a prior generation's spirituality, and to develop rituals that will hold up to the competing interests in the culture.

Congregational change agents face a common systemic dilemma, a loyalty to their forbearers that limits their willingness to confront the systems that are irrelevant for their lives. In families and church families, younger members and innovative new participants are subtly taught that they are disloyal if they achieve more, become happier, or move beyond their parents' notions of church as it once was. Disloyalty to the elders and to their legacy evokes shame. These dynamics motivate subsequent generations to join the prevailing systems of congregational life rather than rocking the boat. Newer members, out of loyalty, may do things the way they've always been done, all the while watching their congregations become grey haired and threatened with extinction. Compliance can be a psychic strategy for younger and newer members of congregations to avoid shame.

Clinging to the past is a shame-avoidance strategy for older and longtime members. Acknowledging the marginalization of congregations in contemporary culture makes room for shame in the gap between what lay leaders and clergy think the congregation should be and the realities of the day. Rather than experience grief over the threatened end of congregational life as it once was, leaders keep their shame at bay by behaving as if nothing has changed or needs to.

One fall I had the opportunity to work with a group of laity from a cluster of churches to help them develop healthy communication patterns in their congregations. The pastor who had invited me was new in his tenure, and he had gotten off to a rocky start. He was incredibly optimistic by nature, however, and he had called in top experts to teach members all that they would need to know to create a vibrant and healthy congregation. Because he was convinced that his congregation was a group of people with great potential, he plunged right in to make changes. He looked at their empty classrooms and said, "Preschool!" He saw their crowded Sunday service and said, "Add another one." He saw their minimal mission outreach and started a food kitchen. In just a few months, members became exhausted trying to keep up with him and started resisting his every idea. One of the laypeople at the workshop was eager to talk about what had happened. He said, "Dr. McClintock, could you please tell our new pastor not to use the *change* word anymore? Every time he says that word, we feel inadequate." Wow. This was a powerful admission.

The pastor, by taking steps to create new ministries had evoked comparison shame. He compared them to some other congregation he'd been to, some old heyday when they were vibrant and growing, or some imagined future they could not yet see. Whenever he said "Change," they heard, "You are not okay the way you are." When he said, "You have *so much* potential," they heard, "You are not living up to your calling" and "You are not doing enough," and they experienced shame. Relationally, he had to learn a different approach. To his credit, he started coaching them with grace instead of shame. He provided far more positive affirmation about their ministry together and asked for their permission to discuss something new. He gave them more choices for how to proceed, and they gained a feeling of having power and control over their changes. This lowered their anxiety that they'd never measure up to his expectations. The congregation grew hopeful and learned to think of themselves as capable of change. Their former attitude of scarcity changed into an attitude of abundance.

Many congregations undermine the work of new clergy from the get-go by implying that they could not possibly ever be as good, capable, tireless, holy as the last one. I was the guest preacher at a church abuzz with excitement over the upcoming tenure of a newly hired pastor. On the day I preached, the new pastor and his wife had just arrived in town and were attending church, even before they unpacked the moving van. Coincidentally, the Gospel lesson from the lectionary described the start of Jesus's ministry in Galilee. I connected these two starting places in the opening of my sermon and used humor to note the comparison shame that often takes place in congregations when parishioners set their expectations for the new pastor a bit too high.

> Our Scriptures today point us to the beginning of Jesus's ministry, and today we also note the beginning of a new pastoral tenure. Herein is my first crucial point. Don't get the new pastor confused with Jesus. He will not walk on water, and he will not turn your grape juice into wine. He will not send the demons inside of your brother into a group of pigs on a ranch and run them off rocks to their deaths. While he is with you, he won't likely have to deal with leprosy, but he will encounter illness and

take a part in healing them. He may not raise anyone from literal death, but there will be little resurrections along the way.
Your new pastor is not Jesus, and he's not God. He will introduce
you to God believing that you and God are capable of developing a healthy and positive relationship. He's more matchmaker
than savior.

I went on to describe the dangers of comparison and offered
them realistic expectations for their ministry together. The new
pastor will not be like the last one, and the new pastor will not be
like the next one. The new pastor will be, by the grace of God,
his own unique self. "During the first year of his ministry," I told
them, "his main task is to love you and to teach you to love him."
Part of that job is always to reduce the presence of comparison
shame.

It would be helpful for a pastor new to a congregation to be
mindful of comparisons as well. Clergy are often tempted to compare their new parish experiences to their previous one or to some
distant idealized congregation they learned about at a recent sem-
inar. They may have come from a terrible experience and think
that telling the new congregation how much better it is will boost
the collective egos of the members. But what actually happens is
that the new people become afraid that some day they too will fall
out of the pastor's good graces. They will become the place he
says is worse than the new place he has gone to. If he keeps saying,
"At Trinity we always did it like this," they will grow tired of trying
to become his previous parish. If he says, "I'm really relieved that
you have only one service on Sunday morning," they will become
immobilized with anxiety when they grow large enough to add
a second. Shame-based comparisons need to be eliminated for
healthy relationships to develop. This principle makes common
sense when you think about people dating again after divorce. A
divorcée who spends time on her first date comparing the new
love interest to her former partner will sabotage the date. A man
who compares the behaviors of his new girlfriend to his previous

one will quickly find himself alone. In the same way, a pastor can ruin a new relationship with comparisons.

A visiting bishop overheard the pastor of one of the congregations in his area expressing comparison shame; the pastor was saying that his congregation wasn't growing as fast as a new megachurch in the conference. Instead of reinforcing the pastor's comparison shame, the bishop carefully and kindly said, "We all share in each other's successes, because we have the same goal of teaching, serving, and creating disciples." Making room for everyone's diverse ways of succeeding lowers comparison shame.

Congregational leaders and clergy have the opportunity of becoming shame-less by lowering comparisons when evaluating clergy. I have seen the egos of clergy devastated when congregations have used overt and covert channels (gossip, rumors, anonymous e-mails) to label and shame them for their deficiencies. In congregations that seek to be shame-less, evaluations focus on mutual or differing goals and the fit between the clergyperson and the congregation. They don't compare their ministry to another congregation's or their clergy to some former guru or idealized other. They look at the goals of the congregation and their pastor and determine ways they can work together to carry out the ministry to which they have all been called. An aboveboard evaluation that focuses on the multiple gifts of clergy and congregants and attempts to recruit skilled individuals to complement the team is a grace-filled and shame-less approach. A nonshaming evaluation process engages curiosity and a desire to know each other's motivations, passions, and priorities. Clergy, staff, and congregational leaders who use the skill of self-definition in tense situations lower shame and increase grace. The unique character of the clergyperson and the congregation are both affirmed and celebrated.

Jesus's disciples, the scholars he taught, and people in crowds often asked him to tell them how to get to the proverbial top of the heap. How will we be sure that we can get into the kingdom? When we sit with God, how can we be sure we're on the "right" side? How can we be the greatest when you tell us we have to be the least? These questions represent more than the vanity of the questioners. They echo the tendency of every human being to strive for certainty and power. But the questions also reflect our fear of rejection, inadequacy, and punishment in this life or in hell. They point us to the phenomenon of comparison shame that I have been describing. The goal of being the best actually leaves us feeling shame for who we aren't rather than joy in who we are. By vying for favor with Jesus, his disciples revealed their underlying fears of lack and inadequacy. Hadn't they heard anything he had said to them? His teaching was so inclusive that he went beyond an accounting of their sins or virtues. He invited everyone. He let all the children come, and he let them be curious! He let all those who were ashamed or had been shamed come, and he gave them honored places. In his grace, we are all welcomed and cherished. No more comparisons needed.

CHAPTER 6

Perfection Shame
Quieting Our Inner Critic

An often misunderstood and misinterpreted saying of Jesus is, "Be perfect, therefore, as your heavenly Father is perfect" (Matt. 5:48). Many individuals have been harmed by ceaseless striving for perfection. This impossible goal is nevertheless still preached from temples on Saturday night and pulpits on Sunday morning. Hebrew Scripture proclaims that we are all created in the image and likeness of God, but when Adam and Eve tried to become like God, they fell out of favor and shame entered the picture. When the people of Babel started building a tower so high they could walk into heaven, they were not rewarded for trying to be like God; they were reminded of their humanity.

You can never be satisfied with yourself if you are constantly striving to be as wise, good, kind, or as generous as God. "You could be *so* much better," says the pastor, the rabbi, or the spiritual teacher, "if you would become more like . . ." Believers in every tradition are bombarded with what I call perfectionist theology. The lie of perfectionist theology is that with sufficient meditation and discipline, you can actually be as perfect as Buddha, Krishna, Allah, Christ, or Yahweh. While we scramble to put our lives together to achieve such glory, we are frequently chided for having missed that mark. Perfectionist theology reinforces the comparison shame we learned in childhood and practice as adults.

Comparing ourselves to God, we can be sure that we will never measure up. Our successes will be fleeting, and our failures will permanently disconnect us from God and one another.

Rabbi and author Harold Kushner in his book *How Good Do We Have to Be?* points to the frustrating futility of perfectionist theology.

> When religion teaches us that one mistake is enough to define us as sinners and put us at risk of losing God's love . . . , when religion teaches us that even angry and lustful thoughts are sinful, then we all come to think of ourselves as sinners, because by that definition every one of us does something wrong, probably daily. If nothing short of perfection will permit us to stand before God, then none of us will, because none of us is perfect.[1]

In one week at my counseling office, I heard a practicing Buddhist, a lapsed Unitarian, and an atheist similarly describing their failure to live up to their "highest" selves. The Buddhist was ashamed of his lack of time commitment to his meditation practice. The Unitarian felt selfish for taking a weekend away from her family for rest and retreat. And the atheist struggled to prove to his boss that he was worthy of the recognition he thought he deserved, while also fearing that he really didn't. A common thread in our humanity is that we experience shame in the space between who we are and the idealized person we strive to be. For people of faith, the striving is reinforced by scriptures on perfection and holiness. So many rules for living the perfect life are set forth in ancient religious texts that no one can possibly adhere to all of them. We end up in a perpetual state of failure, either shaming ourselves or being shamed in our communities of faith. There has to be a more graceful way!

THE JUDGING SUPEREGO

When we frantically aim for perfection, we place ourselves in spiritual and psychological peril. A high school student recently told me that she had gotten a grade of 4.5 in a class. "What?" I asked her, thinking 4.0 was a perfect score. Has the bar been set even higher? A good grade becomes not enough; a better grade becomes the expectation. When the bar is set too high, the joy of accomplishment vanishes, and we experience sadness for not quite reaching a goal. Achievements are trivialized when they are seen only as steps on the way to loftier goals. When the report card comes home, too many students and their parents don't celebrate the B grades because they are not As. Cs aren't even viewed as average any longer. Who wants to be average? Parents who demand great achievements from their children may purposefully resort to shame tactics, believing (mistakenly) that shame is harmless motivation. Years later those adult "kids" sit in my counseling office processing their grief that their parents weren't proud of them, feeling depressed about their lack of success and fed up with having to prove themselves worthy of love and acceptance.

Perfectionism can harm other kinds of relationships too. I bristle when I hear songs on the radio with lyrics that say something like "I'm never going to hurt you," because they are so very unrealistic. In every relationship, there is an element of risk as we become more intimate. The more vulnerably we love, the more we will experience hurt and pain (in small ways, we hope, but sometimes tremendously). If we spend our lives trying to be free of ordinary hurts and pains, we may end up alone and lonely. The perfectionist who either avoids acknowledging his power to hurt others or, conversely, obsessively records his deficits puts up roadblocks to healthy connection. While the perfectionist is busy adding up her mistakes and failures, the people around her will either try to change her opinion about herself or go on without her. Her striving for perfection will leave her feeling frustrated and lonely. I cannot say this often enough. We are not perfect. And that's nothing to be ashamed of.

I have a puppet of Sigmund Freud, the father of psychoanalytic theory, who peers down at me from the bookshelf above my writing desk. He has on a black suit, which contrasts with his huge white eyebrows and little black glasses. He's expressionless and almost cross-eyed as he looks at me while I am writing. I get to imagine whatever I want to about what he is thinking about me. Some days, he's happier than others. Some days he shakes his head, looks at the floor, and blushes with shame.

Freud's theories on the unconscious, developed in the early 1900s, laid the groundwork for future psychological examinations of guilt and shame.[2] In his understanding, the mature self is made up of a trinity of unconscious characters: the id, which is hedonistic, adolescent, and playful; the superego, which is the voice of the parent or other moralistic disciplinarian we hear in our heads to rein in the whims of the id; and the adult ego, which is left with the job of mediating between the other two. He would likely say that my self-critical outbursts while I construct this book are parts of a *judging superego.*

Let me describe the way this works. I am sitting at my desk looking at a copy of this chapter, which has been returned to me by my editor. It is filled with comments and suggestions that I trust explicitly, but my superego mounts an attack that goes something like this: "You're not saying anything new, someone's already said this *better*, and by the way, your readers are going to be bored by this because *you are boring*!" The voice in my head torments me. My judging superego attempts to control me. Like a partner in a long-term marriage, the superego has learned my vulnerability to certain accusations and lets them fly without my overt permission. When I am writing, the superego can lay me flat in less than a paragraph full of sentences. In reality, I am the person who heaps the greatest shame upon my own head by giving my superego the power to shame me. I suspect that you do the same thing to yourself. Unchecked, our superego can get the upper hand. One way the superego undermines our confidence is by focusing on supposedly perfect people we are *not like.* Those people are more together, have fewer problems, are more brilliant, talented, and successful than we are. Sometimes we charge ourselves with the crime of imperfection, create the jury for our own trials, and then, without a defense attorney, convict and sentence ourselves.

The psyche is so good at driving us toward perfection that it sometimes makes up fictional characters who have absolutely none of our problems or flaws. Flora Wuellner, spiritual teacher and author, asks her readers in her book *Release for Trapped Christians* to try an experiment—to close their eyes and imagine a perfect person. Here's Flora's fictional image of a perfect Christian woman:

> She is busier in good works than anybody else, but never seems hurried or flurried! She is calmly efficient and infinitely loving as she takes on everyone else's burdens! She is never tired. She is never cross. She never needs anything for herself. Her voice—never raised in annoyance—rings clear as a bell with authority and wisdom. She has every one of the gifts of the Spirit. She never feels fear or doubt or loneliness or personal longings.[3]

By comparing herself to this ideal Christian woman, Wuellner repeatedly gave her superego the power to shame her. "This lady haunted me pretty persistently for many years. Anything about me that didn't fit into her image was obviously wrong and sinful."[4] Perhaps you have invented a perfect person like this in your own mind.

According to psychoanalytic theory, during maturation we naturally develop the *ego ideal* self alongside the true ego. The ideal self can assist us in dreaming big dreams, aspiring to lofty accomplishments, and planning a satisfying life. But the ideal self frequently shames the real one. In an essay called "Shame: The Underside of Christianity," psychologists John M. Berecz and Herbert W. Helm Jr. describe this disparity. "The ideal self is the repository of dreams, goals, and fantasies of the kind of person one ought to become."[5] The ideal self also sets unachievable expectations, which it gently mocks when it asks rhetorically, "After all, what could be so bad about trying harder? What is wrong with setting high goals? Why not shoot for the stars?"[6] The ideal self sounds incredibly good on the surface.

However, the ideal self takes account of every mistake we have ever made and points out to us that we are perpetually falling short. Berecz and Helm explain why this stern accounting is a problem for us:

> Failure to meet the expectations of the ideal self produces shame, which seldom fosters growth. It is precisely here that we have possibly produced more problems than we have healed because much Christian preaching, writing, and dogma is concerned with raising the ideal self to ever higher levels. . . . The irony is that by attempting to produce better, kinder, purer people, the Christian church has produced more shameful people.[7]

The wider the gap between our ordinary humanity and God, the more ashamed we become. The term *spiritual superego* has come into popular usage to describe the way our overactive superegos can be egged on by teachings from religion. Each religious discipline holds within it the power to reinforce our tongue-lashings. And each religious discipline sets high standards that many of us never reach. Berecz and Helm ask, "How could one find a higher ideal that the Incarnate God?"[8]

Striving for extraordinary saintliness, for messianic greatness, or to obtain immortality will simply leave us exhausted and despondent. This stretch toward self-deification sets up a lifelong gap between the ego and the superego, which have more commonly been called *the real self* and *the ideal self*. That gap leaves us with a constant sense of failure and a perpetual drive to overcome it.

In Jesus's teaching from the Sermon on the Mount, one oft-quoted instruction has typically been translated, "Be ye perfect" (Matt. 5:48). However, the Greek word *teleios,* which is often translated "perfect," is more accurately translated as "whole." The word implies completion and maturity, or in common vernacular, "being full grown." As we become spiritually and psychologically mature, the real self and the ideal self merge into one. The mature ego brings the nagging voice of the superego and the hedonistic drives of the id into harmony within the personality. The spiritual superego is unnecessary, because we have gained spiritual acceptance and become lifelong students who can be okay with average grades. Self-acceptance replaces self-criticism. Grace replaces shame. We learn to accept and even embrace our imperfections. We give up the futile striving that perfectionism demands. We quit trying to be perfect.

When United Methodist clergy are ordained, we say in the ordination service that we are going on to perfection and that we expect to be made perfect in our lifetimes—a presumtuous claim. John Wesley himself admitted that he had known very few people who had achieved it. The drive to be perfect is nevertheless placed on the shoulders of clergy in most denominations. They feel pressured to be righteous, holy, and self-sacrificing, and congregations are inclined to reward these impossible goals. In her memoir *Leaving Church,* preacher and professor of Christian spirituality Barbara Brown Taylor writes of striving for perfection in her career as parish priest.

> For most of my adult life, what I have wanted most to win is nearness to God. This led me to choose a vocation that marked me as God's person both in my eyes and in the eyes of others. I gave myself to the work the best way I knew how, which sometimes exhausted my parishioners as much as it exhausted me. I thought that being faithful meant always trying harder to live a holier life and calling them to do the same. I thought that it meant knowing everything I could about scripture and theology, showing up every time the church doors were open, and never saying no to anyone in need. I thought that it meant ignoring my own needs and those of my family until they went away altogether, leaving me free to serve God without any selfish desires to drag me down.
>
> I thought that being faithful was about becoming someone other than who I was, in other words, and it was not until this project failed that I began to wonder if my human wholeness might be more useful to God than my exhausting goodness.[9]

Taylor is not alone in her striving or her inevitable exhaustion. In moments of fatigue, burnout, and self-defined failure, we are forced to reevaluate the perfection myth.

Before embracing faith as an active and engaging endeavor, many of us originally converted to a religious system with a set of rules that defined how we "should" act and feel. Under these traditional command-and-obedience theologies, generations of believers find their shame reinforced. No wonder, then, that during her ministry Barbara Brown Taylor needed a time of recovery from her ceaseless, perfection-driven striving for holiness. It makes sense that Flora Wuellner had invented a perfect Christian woman after whom to model her life.

We can learn from those who have faced down the demon of their own perfectionism and speak openly about the damage of perfectionism in congregational life and leadership. Wuellner eventually purged that perfect Christian woman from her life by erasing the woman's image from her superego's hard drive. She suggests that to do this requires a life of prayer and letting go. She advises, "Beware of those parts in your self that repress, shout down, [and] ignore other parts of yourself."[10] Acceptance of the whole, as well as acceptance of our unique gifts and foibles, is crucial in becoming shame-free. Wuellner concludes, "We are not to imitate anybody—however noble. . . . We are not even to imitate Jesus, we are to *abide* in Jesus."[11] Each of us is unique, with our own expressions of love, our own behaviors, and our own evolving souls. Welcomed and embraced by God in our wholeness, we no longer need to invent someone else to compare ourselves to or to become.

NARCISSISM: WHEN SHAME GOES INTO HIDING

Unfortunately, it becomes difficult to give up perfectionism when shame goes into hiding. People who look and act like they have it all together often turn out to be the most shame-based on the inside. The more charming and successful they appear to be, the more inadequate they may actually feel. They have covered their shame with hedonism, competitiveness, and success. To keep from feeling their own pain and unworthiness, they develop an alternative persona. This condition, known as narcissism, usually begins in childhood.

Children are naturally self-centered and inclined to draw attention to themselves, which helps them get their needs met. If parents fail at the job of empathetically attending to those needs and demonstrating altruism, their children may remain stuck at a self-centered stage of development. These ashamed children grow up to be self-focused adults, and when they are rejected by others for their egoism, they create an even tougher false exterior. The real self goes into hiding, and a more acceptable idealized exterior self is created within the personality and presented to others for approval. In this condition, the false exterior obscures imperfections. While all of us daily engage in image management, those with narcissistic features do little else. Every word spoken and every feeling expressed is carefully chosen to project a positive self-image.

Psychologists who evaluate the emotional wellness of clergy candidates report that more clergy candidates suffer from narcissism than any other personality disorder. The classification describes people who have "a pervasive pattern of grandiosity, need for admiration, and lack of empathy that begins in early adulthood and is present in a variety of contexts."[12] In the ancient Greek myth about Narcissus, this handsome young god was looking for love in all the wrong places, as they say. He looked into a pool of water one day and fell in love with himself. If only someone would have nudged him from behind so that he could have fallen into the water and gotten over that!

The story of Narcissus describes the excesses of self-love that reduce relationships to flattery of the ego. Individuals with narcissism are not as confident as they seem, not as charming as they appear. They are wounded, like the rest of us, and have created a complex way to mask their flaws. When the ideal self takes over for the real self, fantasies arise about possessing "unlimited success, power brilliance, beauty, or ideal love."[13] A person with narcissism believes that he has a right to use others, to obtain success through ethically questionable means. She can avoid personal responsibility for her anger and rejection of others because she's "above all that." He has a sense of entitlement. She takes advantage of others to present an acceptable self-image, and she manipulates others to keep the idealized self in place.

It makes sense that individuals who have an inordinate amount of shame, or a huge gap between the real and ideal self, enroll in seminary and prepare for a vocation where people ascribe messianic qualities to them. They end up with the power to interpret the word of God, to order the life of God's people, to decide who is shunned by the community and who is sainted. Meanwhile, they assert their right to the admiration and adoration they seek. The person with narcissistic grandiosity does not admit to having or feeling shame and is unable to receive and make use of criticism. Feelings of inadequacy are denied by maintaining the narcissistic defense.

Individuals with narcissism lack an ability to be in compassionate relationships. They have shallow relationships with those who flatter them and become angry and rejecting when others fail to admire them. These individuals see nothing wrong with presenting themselves as Christlike role models. Their audacity helps them to disown their ordinariness and repress their inner shame. They use comparison shame in complex ways to support their superior status. Individuals with narcissistic defenses spend a good deal of time evaluating other people's willingness to support the fragile self they have created. Those who go along with them are flattered and admired, as well, while those who confront them are rejected and shamed.

Not all clergy are categorically narcissistic, but many have similar defense mechanisms that protect them from exposing their character flaws. They seek the assurance (and reassurance) of a group of believers that they are worthy of their calling. Their idealized personalities are mirrored back to them when congregants see them as the perfect parent, leader, healer, and teacher.

NARCISSISTIC CLERGY AND NARCISSISTIC CONGREGATIONS: A (NOT SO) PERFECT MATCH

Perfection-driven clergy are drawn to perfection-driven congregations. They fit together in a (not so) perfect match. It came as a surprise to me as a congregational consultant when I became aware of several congregations that fit most of the diagnostic criteria for individuals with narcissistic disorders. Seeing themselves as *the ideal congregation,* they recruit (or ask the bishop to send them) *an ideal pastor.* Then, the congregation and the pastor can both wear a mask of self-righteousness and join together to disown shame.

To cover over any hint of inadequacy, these congregations and their clergy endeavor to have the best of everything and be the best at everything. They have noteworthy outreach programs and choirs that go on world tours. They have shiny new buildings or meticulously restored ones that reflect their status in the community, about which they take great pride. Programs and people appear to be less valued than the buildings. New member recruitment is limited to those who would enhance the image of the congregation. Clergy and lay leaders in these congregations are driven more by achievement than relationship.

Lay members in narcissistic congregations reinforce the high ego ideals of their clergy. They pay them at levels that exceed those of other clergy in comparably sized congregations. They frequently talk about past preachers, many of whom went on to publish, to teach at well-respected institutions, or to become denominational leaders at the highest levels.

With extremely high expectations for performance standards, ordinary clergy would disappoint the image-driven congregation, leading to conflicts and criticism. Perfectionist clergy set the bar for themselves at exceptionally high levels, and then parishioners come along and raise it even higher. Matched with perfectionist congregations, the partnership is likely to end badly. When clergy fail to produce the best sermons, preside over moving worship experiences weekly, or meet their parishioners at the admitting department of the hospital to provide pastoral care, they receive harsh criticism and even verbal harassment from members. Worse yet, if they become ill, have marital difficulties, or in any way fail to meet the expectations of parish leaders, they are likely to engage in behaviors that will lead to termination or firing. To extricate themselves from psychically dangerous criticism or the unmasking of their perfect presentation of themselves, clergy with narcissistic defense mechanisms may cross interpersonal boundaries, seek solace in sexual affairs, or otherwise engage in misconduct. Narcissistic congregations are more likely than more balanced congregations to have experienced histories of multiple incidents of abuse by their leaders.

Even the brightest and the best clergy can fall (and do) under the pressure of perfectionism while struggling with feelings of unworthiness. If you hear a clergyperson say, "If they only knew . . . ," this may be a person in trouble, serving a congregation in trouble. Ask him or her to call a congregational consultant or a therapist to get help. When you hear congregational leaders talking about a clergyperson abusing them, listen carefully, take them seriously, and urge them to seek intervention from a consultant or judicatory leader. Too often the problem in these situations is defined as one bad clergyperson or a backbiting, critical congregation. These simplified views cannot describe the complexity of the narcissistic defense and perfectionism gone awry. Both clergy and the congregation need intervention.

Conference leaders, bishops, and superintendents can also be narcissistic perfectionists, trying to maintain a respectable public image in the face of embarrassments and gross mistakes. Conferences frequently keep things under wraps, hiring lawyers who support them as they try to protect the institution. Keeping shame from public view can take up time and resources. Efforts to maintain a positive image of the conference, judicatory, or denomination often run roughshod over the needs of clergy and lay members. What is needed is transparency and accountability regarding issues that may be shameful, such as sexual harassment in congregations, clergy and lay staff abuse, embezzlements, clergy incompetence, dying congregations, and denominational decline, rather than scrambling to maintain an image of an ideal institution. Whole conferences hide their histories rather than face and heal their shame. It is time to actively change the culture of perfectionism in which shame hides. Sometimes it takes a major financial settlement following abuse to bring the truth forward and to move an institution toward humility rather than humiliation.

GIVING UP PRETENSES

Like other United Methodist clergy, I sat with my stole over my arm listening to a conference preacher at my ordination service describing the joys and perils of congregational ministry. It was an emotional day for a dozen candidates, and especially so for me in my fifth month of pregnancy. We had all spent years in seminary, spent time working in congregational internships and sitting before committees of our peers, "jumping through hoops" to become ordained. At last I was waiting for my turn to kneel at the communion rail, receive the blessing of friends and colleagues, and be ordained. During the liturgy, using words that had been spoken for decades before me, the bishop asked me if I was going on to perfection and if I expected to be made perfect in this lifetime. I'm rather sure I never hesitated in saying yes.

But since I said those words, I have changed my mind. Because I think not only that perfection is unachievable and unnecessary but also that striving for it is psychologically harmful, I have stopped aiming for it. I aim instead for the right to make mistakes, to be a human among other humans, to learn from my wounds and the wounds I inflict on others, and to give up perpetual striving and self-criticism. This shift leaves me a little shame-less. It moves me from shame to grace.

I had the opportunity to mentor a clergyperson I'll call Sam during his first few years as parish pastor. The congregation in

which he served was midsized and had a relatively stable membership. It was known in the community for hosting the local food
pantry and participating in groundbreaking interfaith dialogue.
He was well liked by the congregation but regularly dissatisfied
with his own ambivalence about pastoral care. In private moments,
he doubted his calling, because making emotional connections
with the people he was serving was hard for him. "Sometimes I just
don't care about their lives," he said. "Sometimes I just wish I was
home reading a book or enjoying my own family." He interpreted
these feelings as personal inadequacies, because he had set up an
idealized picture in his mind of the way caring clergy are supposed
to be. The more Sam felt bored with his work and disconnected
from his people, the more he put in long hours and neglected
himself and his family. It didn't occur to him that the disconnection was a sign that he might have been doing too much, that he
really did need time at home, or that he was overwhelmed by the
amount of work a clergyperson could or should do when serving a
congregation of five hundred people. Sam's idealized self pressed
him to do more, be more, feel more, and in response, the real
self (and perhaps an endearing rebel boy inside him) decided to
just check out of the emotional relationships that had become so
draining.

To overcome the predicament, Sam had to acknowledge that
his disconnection from the people of the parish was a disconnection inside himself. He disconnected to avoid shame, which
he experienced in the form of self-criticism and criticism by his
parish leaders. When he took time away from the parish for the
self-care he desperately needed, people resented his "withdraw-
als" and acted as if he had abandoned them. As he explored his
shame about letting either himself or the parish down, he realized
that he needed a new approach. Recognizing that he *wanted* to
be his true self in relationships with others, he explored ways to
talk about the needs of the parish and his needs with his personnel committee and key leaders. When tired, he needed to rest.
When bored, he needed to join his family for laughter and play.
When overworked, he needed to work less, not more. To help him

integrate his adult self and his ashamed little boy, I had him spend a few weeks between our conversations thinking of himself as ordinary. I encouraged him to ask himself, "What would an ordinary person feel right now? What would an ordinary person want, do, say?" The exercise provided him with a reflective distance between his idealized self and his ordinary self. Once he accepted his ordinariness, he could balance service with replenishment and engagement with separation. The shame fell to the wayside, and he began to live in grace. Facing his shame and his attempts to flee from it by creating a superman self helped Sam to become integrated and whole, which reflected the true meaning of Jesus's teachings on perfection. He gradually lightened his load and felt a joy he hadn't allowed himself for years.

Sam's experience isn't uncommon. A friend of mine sent me a funny synopsis that was being passed around on the Internet on the perfectionist expectations of clergy and their congregations, and I've shortened it and made it inclusive for our purposes. *The Perfect Pastor* preaches exactly fifteen minutes—and condemns sin roundly but never hurts anyone's feelings. *The Perfect Pastor* works from 8:00 a.m. until midnight and is also the church janitor. *The Perfect Pastor* makes forty dollars a week, wears great clothes, drives an eco-friendly car, buys and reads the latest books, and gives half of his or her salary back to the church. *The Perfect Pastor* is twenty-nine years old and has forty years of experience. *The Perfect Pastor* has a burning desire to work with teenagers and spends all day with senior citizens. *The Perfect Pastor* smiles all the time while being seriously dedicated to the congregation. *The Perfect Pastor* makes fifteen home visits a day and is always in her office in order to be available when needed. This humorous look at pastoral ministry became popular on the Internet because it is so painfully true. It's clearly time to stop expecting clergy to be perfect. Clergy need to focus more on health and wholeness and less on perfection. What do they need to be? Not perfect. Shame-less.

I'm impressed by the fact that in the natural world, things are perfectly imperfect. Creation is wonderful, and it is not technically perfect. No two snowflakes are alike. The avocado has a rather large pit for its overall size. Things aren't plumb, the horizon curves, straight lines are hard to come by. So why is it that we expect a different kind of perfection in ourselves or other people? We have limitations; we are fallible. Accepting this fact moves us toward growth and satisfaction. Denying this leaves us in constant effort to cover up, press down, and destroy aspects of ourselves we deem to be unacceptable. This process is extremely tiresome and leads only to sadness, depression, and isolation. To counter the voice of perfection, we need to love and accept the fullness of our real selves and to avoid the traps of creating unrealistically ideal selves. Less perfection leads to less shame, and becoming shame-less will open our souls to the amazing richness of God's accepting grace.

Some of you, having grown accustomed to shame, may need one more cautionary paragraph. You cannot move toward grace by berating yourself for having a bit of narcissism. Nor will it help you to feel ashamed of your congregation or denomination for its harmful habit of trying to look good at the expense of healthy relationships. Take a deep breath and resist the shame-blame pattern I have described. Narcissistic features in personalities serve as defense mechanisms to keep shame at a safe distance. When shame is named for what it is, narcissism is healed. Individual clergy, lay leaders, and congregations begin to engage in healthier interaction patterns. They no longer need to present themselves falsely.

Perfectionism is a misguided defense against shame. Learning about the dangers and damages of perfectionism simply allows us to notice that old strategy for what it is and to eliminate it. It's time for us to realize, as Barbara Brown Taylor did, that God needs our wholeness more than our perfection. The masks we wear to make ourselves look good aren't needed any longer. The exhausting, endless striving becomes unnecessary. By accepting ourselves and others as people who are not better or worse, just good enough, we become shame-less. We give up the old defensive strategies and move into wholeness, humility, and grace.

CHAPTER 7

Chronic Illness Shame
Community Is the Cure

Transferring from doctor to doctor, Rhonda found little help for her chronic pain. She went to a naturopath, an acupuncturist, a primary care physician, an internist, a pain specialist, a physical therapist, and a surgeon. These medical providers held widely divergent views on the cause of the problem and how to treat it. Her primary doctor said, "It's a mystery." Not certain what he was treating, he nevertheless wanted to relieve her suffering and prescribed her numerous pain medications. Thereafter, she was accused by her internist of drug seeking, and he became even less likely to pay attention to her cries for help. "There's nothing more I can do for you" was a line she became used to hearing. Rather than relax on her vacation, she visited an out-of-state pain specialist for yet another opinion. That consultation turned out to be the most difficult of all: the pain specialist told her that her physical pain was common among women who "spend their lives serving others and never taking care of themselves." In other words, she was told, her condition was the result of her codependent behavior and therefore her own fault.

Rhonda became spiritually defeated. She prayed, but her words seemed to float into the void. When her name appeared on the list of people to pray for in the congregation's newsletter, she was more embarrassed than grateful. She went to church less and less often to avoid anyone asking how she was doing.

Rhonda's insurance company became concerned about her medical costs and assigned her a kind caseworker to "coordinate care." Unfortunately, he also informed her that the company was reducing her benefits and increasing her out-of-pocket share. As she ran out of stamina and money, she became more and more frustrated and fatigued. A pervasive sadness arose in her, along with other symptoms of depression. At that point her primary care doctor, who had not found a cause or a cure, concluded that the problem was psychological and sent her to a therapist.

Well-meaning friends and family grew weary of Rhonda's moods and pain. "She's just attention seeking," her aging mother said, missing the times when Rhonda used to visit and give her ample time and care. Her friends disappeared, unable to cope with Rhonda's disheartenment. Her hopes of finding a partner with whom to share her future faded over the course of the illness as she felt more and more unworthy. "Who would ever want to be around me?" she queried. "I'd only bring someone else down with me." She isolated herself at home, and the more she did this, the more depressed she became. At this point in her downward cycle, she began to suffer from a condition that isn't officially listed among psychological disorders—an acute shame disorder.

Despite advances in modern medicine, presuppositions about Rhonda's illness frequently led to the conclusion that she was to blame for it. People around Rhonda expressed this blame in very sophisticated ways, but they nevertheless played the blame-shame game. Like people in ancient times, when medical causes were unknown, Rhonda was rendered "unclean." People kept their distance from her to avoid catching a spiritual disease or being overtaken by the demons of hopelessness and despair. While Rhonda's physical condition was presumably not contagious, she and others believed that her crippling sadness could also debilitate the people around her.

LEARNED HELPLESSNESS

The term *learned helplessness* describes a condition in which a person's frustrated attempts to get his or her needs met leads the person to give up. Martin Seligman and others discovered that when animals encountered conditions over which they had no control, they gave up attempts to change the situation and "seemed to develop the animal equivalent of depression."[1] Lab animals were prohibited from reaching food that they could see but not obtain, and it didn't take long before they stopped trying. Eventually, even when the food was made easily available, the animals still didn't try to reach for it. They had learned helplessness.

Subsequent studies have shown that people become depressed and helpless when they feel they have too little control over the stress in their lives. Even thinking that you have no options can cause a drop in mood and decline in functioning. Learned helplessness closely parallels shame. "I can't," "I'll just fail again," "I'm unworthy to ask again," and "I don't deserve it" are some of the persistent cognitive assertions of shame. In learned helplessness, shame is the emotional weight underlying inaction.

Those who suffer from chronic mental or physical illnesses experience several types of shame, which I have described in previous chapters. Comparison shame arises when people with chronic illness compare the life they once had to the one they now have. They dread the future, because further decline in functioning may be inevitable. They compare their own lives to the more active or the healthier lives of others, sometimes resenting the happiness and well-being of loved ones. These dynamics make it difficult for them to remain in loving connection with others.

THE BLAME-SHAME GAME

Searching for the source of the problem, sufferers, their loved ones, and their physicians try to overcome the unknown by placing blame. Sufferers look back over their lives to determine the probable causes of the illness, whether or not they are logical. Rhonda might focus on the time she spent working around paint fumes or heavy chemicals in a furniture factory or cleaning her own bathroom with toxic products. She might fret about a diet filled with food additives and too few green vegetables. She might think about the amount of alcohol she consumed, the drugs she experimented with, the recklessness of her early years, her prior callousness about her own health. This self-incrimination is a commonly used version of the blame-shame game.

Once she has conducted an inventory of her own likely contributions, she could take the blame elsewhere. The medical community could be targeted for their incompetence, providing incorrect diagnoses, prescribing medications with undisclosed side effects. There's plenty of blame to mask the shame of chronic illness.

In a support group for people with chronic pain, participants express blame toward their families. "If only I hadn't worked so hard to provide for them," a man with chronic back pain asserts. "My husband expected me to sacrifice my health to care for his dying mother," a woman with fibromyalgia bemoans. The chronically ill mother of an adult daughter concludes, "Stress about my daughter's job layoff led to this problem." When human error fails to completely satisfy the anger and frustration of illness, God is blamed too.

How the person handles the illness is another source of shame. If family members and friends see "giving into it" as counterproductive, they may push their weakened loved one beyond self-imposed or medically determined limits. Encouraging them to buck up, family members may be unrealistic about activities and engagements, which can lead to relational cutoffs and resentments. Fearing that he is disappointing others, the sufferer isolates himself. To avoid the pressures of friends, family, and faith communities, he withdraws. More and more self-hatred grows as the one who is ill cancels social engagements, postpones trips, leaves phone calls unreturned. This downward spiral leads into depression and loneliness. It all adds up to a chronically ill person's fixed belief in his or her own unworthiness.

ILLNESS SHAME IN THE GOSPELS

Chronic mental and physical illness shame appears frequently in the Gospels. The dynamic of learned helplessness is at play in the biblical story of Jesus's encounter with a man who was lying by the pool near the Sheep Gate, waiting for someone to put him in the water. From time to time the water was swirled and churned by an angel, and thereafter the first person to enter it was healed (John 5:2–18). Many individuals who were blind, lame, and paralyzed were waiting at the water's edge. The man who caught Jesus's attention that day had been there for thirty-eight years. That was a "long time" as the narrator suggests—a very long time indeed. It was long enough to lose a family, be reduced to begging for food, experience hopelessness, and learn helplessness. Had he given up trying to get in the pool? Had he come to believe that he was unworthy of healing?

Jesus wisely questioned the man's capacity for change. "Do you want to be made well?" Jesus asked. Did the man desire a different life, or had he utterly lost hope? Was he stuck in his role as victim? "Sir," he said to Jesus, "I have no one to put me into the pool when the water is stirred up; and while I am making my way, someone else steps down ahead of me." Jesus circumnavigates the man's frustration and helplessness by providing a shame-less option: "Stand up, take your mat and walk." The man amazingly trusts this instruction and is immediately healed—no longer stuck, no longer a victim, no longer helpless.

The ancient belief was that the man could not be healed without the interventions of angels, a pool of churned-up water, and the physical ability to push himself to the brink and plunge in. In this beautiful story, we find a different approach. We find a man with a lifelong illness who was noticed. He wasn't just one of the crowd; he was an individual with great suffering, and Jesus made no judgment about his condition. Jesus simply sought to understand it. Within this empathetic connection, the two of them find the necessary steps for the man's healing. This is a story of grace replacing shame.

Jesus's unusual approach toward those who suffer disrupted the blame-shame game of the teachers and healers of his day. The Scriptures abound with stories of individuals overcoming chronic illness because they encounter him. Along with the man who lived by the pool, we find others with long-term suffering: a woman with twelve years of constant bleeding (Mark 5:25–34), a bent-over woman who had "a spirit that had crippled her for eighteen years" (Luke 13:10–11), a man with a demon who had lived his whole life in the tombs (Mark 5:1–20), and a whole host of additional characters with incurable illness, demon possession, or both, resulting in stigma, isolation, and shame.

Observing Jesus's compassion for those around him teaches us to adopt shame-less attitudes toward friends, loved ones, and people in our faith communities. Walking with his disciples, Jesus's attention was quickly drawn to a woman who touched his garment. Shamed and ashamed due to her twelve-year battle with unending menstrual hemorrhaging, she nonetheless reached out to him. As a menstruating woman, she was ritually unclean and could not touch others without rendering them unclean as well. Still, she pushed her way through a crowd and took the risk of making Jesus unclean in order to receive his healing. He also took risks in this story—the risk of publically declaring himself unclean by acknowledging her touch. He admitted that she had touched him, he honored her claim for healing, and he taught his appalled disciples to let go of their fear of catching her shame.

In a story unique to Luke's Gospel, we find Jesus's encounter with the unnamed woman whom commentators frequently refer to as the bent-over woman (Luke 13:10–11). Publically ostracized, through no choice of her own, she inherits the ancient stigma of other bent-over women—mythic hags, crones, and witches, all of them hunchbacked and crippled. She is viewed as a threat to those who are well. Her physical condition is likely the result of back ailments, weakened and breaking bones, and it probably caused her a great deal of pain (without any help from analgesics). Consider as well that the emotional condition of shame is often manifested in the sufferer's posture as a rounded-over back, rolled shoulders, and downcast eyes. The posture of shame is upon her. Perhaps this is why Jesus notices her, perhaps she has emotionally touched him. He goes near her; he touches her; he heals her.

Still in the habit of shame, the disciples play the blame-shame game when they encounter a man born blind, but Jesus will have none of it (John 9:1–7). "Who sinned," they ask him, "this man or his parents?" The blindness is no one's fault, and no one sinned, Jesus asserts, and the disciples are stunned. Freed from the taunts of his neighbors, the curse of the priest, and the fear of strangers, the man sees the world in a whole new way. He not only receives his sight but he also receives the insight necessary to let go of any lingering blame for his years of illness. Before his literal sight is restored, he hears the gracious and merciful message that no one, *no one*, sinned. He becomes shame-less.

When we read these stories, we tend to focus on the miracles of physical healing. But breaking someone out of his or her shame is no small miracle, no less powerful than Jesus's sending demonic spirits into pigs who plunge to their deaths in the sea. Freeing a woman from social stigma is no less significant than straightening the legs of a lame man. These were not puny miracles. From my viewpoint, Jesus's power to lift shame would have been healing enough, regardless of the physical miracles that were also evident.

From these stories we can learn the power of lifted shame. Each person whom Jesus healed was also restored to community. When Jesus frees the man born blind from isolation and restores his sight, shame is taken off the man and his family. The leper goes back to his house of worship, a man gains back his daughter, the woman with the flow of blood becomes literally and ritually clean and returns to her family and friends. These joyful reunions are celebrated throughout the texts, with miracles continuing "offstage" at the end of these stories.

RESTORING HOPE AND HEALING

In Gospel stories where long-term illness is overcome, the cure includes destigmatization and restoration of the sufferer to relationships in which he or she can love and be loved. Researcher and storyteller Brene Brown, in a lecture on the power of vulnerability, defines shame as "the fear of disconnection."[2] The cure for shame, therefore, implies restorative connection. When supportive connections take place, healing extends beyond the physical to the psychological and spiritual. As we examine the role that congregations and other support groups can play in the healing of those with chronic illnesses, we find Brown's theory repeatedly affirmed. Community holds the power to cure.

One way mentally ill individuals and their families can reduce stigmatization and shame is to share their experiences with others. The National Alliance for the Mentally Ill (NAMI)[3] is a nationwide program that overcomes the isolation commonly experienced by family members and friends by providing education and support. These families have often grown exhausted in their searches for cures. They have felt the sting of social rejection that their loved ones endure, and they too end up with helplessness and shame.

Parents may feel intense feelings of guilt about raising a child who becomes mentally ill. Because of this guilt, they may overfunction on behalf of adolescent or adult children with mental illness. Parents have a hard time finding the middle ground between taking on too much responsibility and letting go of all connection and terminating the relationship. What they find in NAMI groups is a safe place to seek this middle ground. Participants share their struggles and openly discuss their sadness about interventions that failed, a lack of available public services, and the high costs of treatment. They gain advice from others, and become shame-less.

Families with mentally ill loved ones who have not found support groups may hide their shame. It was my habit as a congregational pastor to make home visits and to have those visits scheduled by a volunteer. After about a year as the new pastor of a congregation, I realized that one of the families in the picture directory had never scheduled a visit. They brushed off the volunteer's repeated invitations to set up an appointment for me. I phoned them myself, knowing that they would be less likely to dodge my request for a visit, and a few weeks later I sat with Marge and Henry (not their real names, of course) in the living room of their home.

In the middle of our conversation Marge gasped, and there in the doorway stood a tall, pale, and handsome thirty-year-old man I had never seen before. "This is our son Mike," she said with nervousness. "Oh, is he home for a visit?" I naively inquired. "No," she said, looking at the floor and blushing with shame. "He lives upstairs in our house, always has, always will." She asked him to say hello, and he backed up a step to avoid shaking my hand. He muttered a soft "Hello" and quickly headed up the stairs. I said, "Nice to meet you," as he retreated, and that was all. Henry said, "Well, where were we?" as if nothing had taken place, implying that we would pick up the conversation again just where we had left off. We chatted lightheartedly about the church choir and the new organist and never afterward spoke about Mike. But I never stopped wondering about him. I had no experience to draw upon as I searched for ways to ask them questions and offer empathy. Using the language of family systems psychology, I "joined" their family system and kept the pact of silence. But I still wish that I had been courageous enough, or skilled enough, to ask Marge and Henry to tell me more about Mike—to ask an open-ended question such as, "What is it like to have Mike living with you?" or even, "Is there anything that I could do or that our congregation could do to support Mike and to support you in caring for him?" This would have brought us all out of shame and silence.

Certainly most congregations have someone like Mike within their family or friendship circles as well as parents like Marge and Henry. Faith communities, by utilizing their structural connectedness, can reduce social stigma for families facing mental and physical illness and provide them with acceptance and support. Healthy congregations offer restorative relationships for those who have lost peers at work, suffered broken friendships, and endured strained family ties. By making healing connections, laity and clergy can reduce the number and duration of mental health symptoms that accompany illness and seclusion. For individuals with chronic illness and their caregivers, home visits are more than perfunctory appointments on a clergyperson's calendar. They provide mental and physical health lifelines.

Congregations need clergy who have sufficient training in psychology and practical theology in seminary to understand families like Marge and Henry's and who have both the courage and the confidence to speak openly with them. Congregation members can also learn to talk about the people in their pews and those who are homebound in ways that reduce stigma and shame. They can actively seek out and host community-based support groups that foster healing.

The power of healing in communities that care is well documented. Researchers conducted a fifty-year study of a close-knit Italian American village—Roseto, Pennsylvania—to determine why individuals who lived there were physically healthier than people in nearby communities. Residents behaved in many of the same ways as people of any other community—drinking, smoking cigarettes, working in stressful situations, eating fatty foods. The difference in their physical and mental health, known as the Roseto effect, turned out to be the result of the strong sense of community and love they had for one another due to their connections to one another over three generations. Neighbors, extended families, and even newcomers in Roseto were committed to caring for one another, were loyal to each other, and provided love and support at critical times in each other's lives, all of which greatly reduced stress and led to overall improved physical and mental health.[4] Congregations create a similar Roseto effect through outreach in times of illness. Providing transportation to events, making home visits, laying on hands in prayer, and offering lay ministry partnerships with people who are homebound all serve to mitigate against the shame that further isolates people who are ill.

A Cautionary Note

Most faith communities struggle to accept those who appear to be different, and it is not uncommon for people in faith communities to add to people's shame during times of illness. Individuals suffering from mental illness and their family members often experience more shame than grace within their Bible study groups, from their home visitation teams, and from clergy. Religious leaders, engaging in the blame-shame game, have used theology to stigmatize those who suffer from long-term mental and physical illnesses. Depression has been viewed as the result of a lack of faithfulness. Chronic pain has been seen as the fault of the person who cannot or does not turn to God for healing, who does not pray enough, confess enough, or repent enough. If she had a better spiritual walk, she'd be healed, or so the thinking has gone. "Just give it over to God" is a phrase that accuses the sufferer of faithlessness. Far too many people still believe that God sends illness as a way to test the recipient's faith or that Satan brings on illness and pain as a trial to be born with dignity. These messages make people feel powerless and crushed under the weight of "the devil's spell." It leaves the sufferer in the role of victim, even less likely to find grace and healing.

People with long-term problems need to hear that they can live with their illnesses without being overwhelmed by them. Instead, people with anxiety disorders have been told by clergy and friends that they "just have too little trust in God." They have been admonished with lines from Scripture, such as "Therefore I tell you, do not worry about . . . what you will eat or what you will drink, or about your body" (Matt. 6:25). While this is sage wisdom for those with minimal daily worries, the text wasn't likely intended for those with acute or chronic anxiety. Modern science has discovered many underlying physical causes of anxiety, such as thyroid imbalances, blood sugar overloads, folic acid absorption issues, caffeine overdosing, and vitamin D3 deficiencies. Researchers have identified genetic markers for anxiety and anxious depression. Both of these mood disorders have similar neurobiological manifestations. Many depressed people are debilitated by amotivational syndrome, a condition that makes taking even a first step toward a goal overwhelming. Changes in the brain at the onset of anxiety and depression result in lack of interest, inertia, and motivation. While the overlapping dynamics of physiology and psychology remain somewhat mysterious, we have enough information to rule out sin and faithlessness as primary causes of mental illness.

Faith communities foster misconceptions about mental illness. We haven't fully eradicated the idea that sin is the cause, and faith is the cure, of all illness, though we are perhaps more sophisticated in disguising our judgments. We make generalizations about the causes of illness and overlook the courage and faithfulness of sufferers as they find ways to make life as good as possible in the midst of physical pain or mental anguish.

It is not uncommon for clergy and lay ministers to contribute to the shame of those who are physically or mentally ill. Unconvinced by research on the causes of mental illness or ignorant thereof, many clergy dissuade congregants from seeking help. They assert that going to a therapist or to a doctor for medication to treat mental illness shows a lack of trust in the healing power of God.

Clergy are also resistant to addressing the needs of people with chronic illness due to their own level of burnout. As I gather with clergy on retreats and at conferences I often hear them complaining heartily about lists of shut-ins they should visit who are part of their older congregations. Their lack of training in dealing with chronic illness, along with the scarcity of time due to the demands of programs, preaching, and administration, leave many clergy frustrated and burdened. Clergy who face their own exhaustion, depression, or chronic illnesses may especially avoid people with similar conditions due to the power of the negative transference, that is, their own fears about aging, illness, and death. Unlike Jesus's first disciples whose ministry was entirely out where the people were—with the sick, the dying, the crowds of people on hillsides and lakeshores—too many pastors and lay leaders remain focused on those who are active and well. Developing a ministry of outreach and healing beyond the walls of the church or synagogue is essential. At a worship service I recently attended, I noticed this hopeful reminder at the bottom of the bulletin: "Our *worship* is ended, let the *service* begin."

Compassionate clergy, Stephen ministers, and others in pastoral care have learned to suspend judgment toward those who are chronically ill and those who are homebound. They understand the difficulty of social engagement for those who are ill. They avoid prescribing cures, such as telling a homebound person to come back to church or to become active in a study group or program, particularly if these have already been tried. They recognize that like the man at the edge of the healing waters, many sufferers experience their failed attempts as demoralizing shame.

A grace-giving parishioner, rabbi, or pastor encourages others to talk freely about suffering, build trust in connecting with others, and overcome the fear of being stigmatized in order to stay in or return to fellowship. At times of illness, congregations can assist individuals and families with financial resources for co-pays and low cost counseling, helping them to find the healing they need and deserve.

An interim pastor was overheard to say that he didn't see it as his job to build relationships during his tenure at a congregation. I cannot imagine what else he thought he should be doing. Jesus's ministry was entirely built upon relationships. He wasn't sitting behind his desk, he wasn't typing up the liturgy, he wasn't raising funds for the work they were doing. He was connecting with people. In most instances, he didn't stop to find out if they would be good for his cause, either, or if they could harm him with their lack of propriety. Nor did he tell them they had to be "clean" before he would deal with them. This commitment to cherish others *as they are* forms the basis of any healing ministry.

For some time while I was serving a church in a small town, I provided a good deal of pastoral counseling. A woman in our community had stopped attending church because she was suffering from agoraphobia, a crippling fear of leaving home. As her condition progressed, it cost her a job and cut her off from friends, family, and the congregation. I phoned her to learn more about her condition, and intuitively, rather than plan a visit to her home, I offered her an appointment date and time at my office. She balked. She said, "I can't go out *at all* these days; I'm too afraid." With more luck than training, I said, "Well, why don't you bring your fear in here, so I can meet it." She said, "Really?" I said she could bring her terror with her, and she could shake, sweat, and breathe hard. She could curl up on the loveseat in my office or hide under the blanket I keep there. I promised my acceptance of her and her condition. I offered grace for her shame. It got her out the door. Too many times people think that they must be well, whole, or have their act together before they can join a faith community. Perhaps they have never been welcomed just as they are.

Attentive clergy and congregations may be the first to notice signs of a parishioner's declining health by tracking people's worship attendance or withdrawal from activities. When Brenda stopped attending her women's circle, she said it was because she was too busy to attend, but she had actually stopped going after several people repeatedly ignored her whenever she talked about her chronic pain. Others told her that she'd get better if she would confess her sins and repent. She was offended by their comments, so she went on at length, defensively describing her multiple physical problems. Eventually circle members stopped asking her how she was or telling her she was missed in the group.

Brenda and her friends had set up a negative affective loop system. Here's how it worked. When she felt judged by them, she tried to prove her case by lengthy explanations of her suffering. When they heard her go on ad nauseam, they stopped listening and changed the subject. Their silence had negatively reinforced her talking behavior. But because she felt invalidated by this response, she withdrew. Brenda was unconsciously trying to find partners in misery. She had grown up with family members who connected to each other through mutual suffering and had learned that she would get attention from loved ones only if she was in pain. She was unconsciously trying to recreate her family dynamic within the group. But because the group was unaware of the pattern, they didn't know how to approach it differently. No one was at fault in this loop system, but they needed to change it in order to stay connected.

The leaders of the group and the congregation's pastor got together to discuss ways to make their group a more positive environment for everyone. They had quite a discussion about what needed to be done about "the Brenda problem." The old adage "Misery loves company" was mentioned, but it turns out to be flawed. Newer research has shown that misery actually loves *miserable* company. Some members of the group argued that they could help Brenda by listening to her as long as she needed to vent. But that approach, research indicates, doesn't help anyone. Venting has proven to increase negative emotions in the one who is venting, and it circumvents actions that could lead to solutions. Letting others vent is not only counterproductive, in some situations it is also harmful. Joining her misery or letting her vent would be harmful to both Brenda and the group.

Some members of the group argued that they should just let her drop out, because she was unhappy with the group anyway. They felt relief at that idea, because they were experiencing compassion fatigue and had reached the limit of their capacity to be empathetic. Besides, sometimes her stories came too close to home. Listening to Brenda's prolonged agony, they relived their own experiences with illnesses. They recalled a manipulative mother, an alcoholic brother, or a friend whose mental illness led her to take her own life. These overlapping emotional dynamics led otherwise caring people to back away from Brenda's pain. To sit with her while she suffered, they would have to pay attention to and learn from their own emotional responses.

Being part of a church environment where you are supposed to be polite and suspend judgment, group members felt a little reluctant to express their negative feelings about Brenda and her behaviors. Eventually, with rugged honesty, they admitted that judging her distracted them from their personal fears of becoming similarly ill or disabled. They confessed that they were not, after all, very different from Brenda. And once they did that, their hearts were turned toward healing.

They planned to create a healthier group dynamic. They would start each meeting with five minutes of sharing by each person for personal updates and prayer requests. Brenda would have five minutes in which to receive their empathy, rather than strive the whole time to gain their sympathy. Then, throughout the rest of the meeting, they would intentionally focus their conversations on positive aspects of their lives and those of their loved ones, influencing her to do the same. If she showed signs of dropping out again, they would urge her to stay in the group and adhere to the new plan. Since they had themselves become shame-less, they could offer her unlimited grace.

Change the Language, Change the Perspective

As advocates for individuals and families with mental and physical illness, congregations play a key role in reducing shame by using shame-free language. Over the past few decades, counselors, medical providers, and media spokespeople have been reducing shame for those with chronic illness by changing the way we talk about people and their conditions. This is accomplished by a slight shift in wording. Instead of referring to someone by the name of their illness, we now identify them as a person with an illness. For example, rather than say, "He's a schizophrenic," we say, "He's a person with schizophrenia," and instead of saying, "She's manic depressive," we say, "She's a person with bipolar illness." This shame-less approach asserts that people *have* certain conditions; they have not *become* those conditions. A person can have a happy life and suffer from an anxiety disorder. A person can experience acute depression and not become disabled. Health-care providers have dropped the term *invalid* because of its heavy dose of shame. Theologians can do the same. Everyone is valid. It's time that congregations change such nomenclature too. It's about more than being politically correct; it's about becoming shame-less.

Recovery programs are also rethinking their nomenclature in order to reduce shame. Congregations have been instrumental in helping people with addictions by hosting Twelve Step programs. Most of these support groups for people with lifelong addictions to alcohol, gambling, overeating, drug use, and overspending meet free of charge in church parlors, fireside rooms, and basements. The Twelve Step model has proven to be a highly successful intervention for drug and alcohol addictions over the past fifty years. It has changed countless lives for people with addiction as well as their partners and children. But embedded in the model is a shame label I hope will someday change. In overcoming denial about substance use, people at the meetings introduce themselves to one another by saying, "Hi, I'm Ted, and I'm an alcoholic" (sex addict, shopaholic, and the like). It's a label that sticks for the rest of the person's life. The fixed identity that follows the use of the term *addict* can become a dodge of personal responsibility for growth and change. One small shift in thinking would be to say instead, "Hi, I'm Ted, and I suffer from the disease of alcoholism." The addiction may be curable; it may require a lifelong battle for sobriety. But Ted is a *person* with a disease; he is not the disease.

Because these addictive diseases have a great deal of shame attached to them, the change in nomenclature from "I'm an addict" to "I'm a person with an addiction" can enhance esteem and motivate healing. When I talk with family members about problem drinking, they avoid the label *alcoholic*. Who wants to think that mother is an alcoholic? But if I ask if she drinks to a level that concerns them, they will say yes and more readily seek help. Calling mother an alcoholic reinforces shame and secrecy. Saying she has a serious and dangerous disease opens the door for healing.

Addictive behaviors arise from and are followed by shame, and to eradicate the shame, people with addictions avoid these feelings by using again, using more, using more frequently. More shame arises when family members suffer, loved ones become accusatory or leave the relationship, or financial and legal problems come along as a result of the use. People in addictions recovery often come to therapy because they have extremely low self-esteem and feel overwhelming shame.

After years in recovery some people are proud to wear the label of *addict* or *alcoholic* as a sign of the strength of their recovery and the fact that they've given their life to their higher power. Using these terms in the early stages of intervention, however, may simply reinforce shame and denial. Full recovery requires a shift in thinking. The person with the addiction eventually comes to believe that his condition is not a failure of moral or spiritual character (shameful); it is a mental and physical disease that can be overcome (graceful).

Congregations need education about the shame that hovers around addictions in order to help and heal. When we stigmatize individuals, calling them by the names of their diseases, they quickly drop out of our faith communities. As one woman put it, "I couldn't possibly show up in church. I was too ashamed." Bringing in speakers and opening conversations about addictions can produce shame-less fellowships.

A pastor who had a history of alcohol addiction told her congregation about her recovery during her first sermon. As the cliché goes, "You could hear a pin drop." She told her recovery story with self-acceptance and grace and opened the way for a fruitful ministry in the healing of addicted people. Long-held family secrets were revealed to her, and teens heading down dangerous paths confessed to her.

Ministry to people with addictions doesn't require personal experience with or recovery from an addiction. Clergy can interview and recruit community intervention specialists to be on standby for individuals and families who seek help. When weekly prayers during worship recognize personal struggles with addictions, people will talk more openly with clergy and others about their problems. Any willingness to bring the shame of addiction out into the light of grace leads others to freedom as well.

Hands-on Courage

The work of healing takes many diverse forms in courageous congregations. Following Jesus's example, leaders and members don't view chronic illness as an impediment to participation; they view it as an opportunity for connection. While not everyone can be made physically well, most people with chronic illnesses can live well, love deeply, and find meaning and purpose in their lives. Some of the most physically challenged people I have met have been the most resilient.

In one small town congregation, a humble group of people have committed to a ministry they call "healing hands." At the request of congregants, the pastor, nurses at skilled nursing facilities, or social workers in the community, participants in the healing hands ministry meet with those who are sick. They pray, and they lay on hands. One day a week, they schedule appointments with people to meet with them in a room at the church. Those who are sick in body or spirit can come in for healing touch and prayer. Several people are always present to ensure everyone's safety, and touch is carefully offered only at the recipient's request. Their ministry of prayer and healing provides comfort and hope, and is also richly rewarding for them. They are walking in the steps of Jesus.

Proactive clergy and other leaders will call out people within their congregations who can develop ministries such as this one to relieve suffering. Finding and using local resources, they can heal chronic illnesses by hosting groups, providing education and visitor training, reducing shameful language, and reaching out to those who have withdrawn due to physical or mental suffering. The shame-less connection is vital. Community is the cure.

CHAPTER 8

Naked and Ashamed
Reducing Individual Sexual Shame

Of all the forms shame takes, sexual shame is the most pervasive and emotionally devastating. Perhaps the look on your mother's face when she caught you "in the act" is seared in your memory. Maybe when you look in the mirror, you repeat a lover's critical comment about your body. Or try as you might, you find it hard to erase the memory of a night you'd rather forget. You have probably been in sexual situations that you just wouldn't want to talk to anyone about. These are common occurrences.

Why does sexual behavior lead to more shame than other experiences? Our sexuality encompasses many aspects of self-identity, such as physical attractiveness, relational intimacy, and emotional vulnerability. A satisfying sexual encounter requires an ability to physically express feelings and sensations as they arise. As Mae West said, "Sex is emotion in motion."[1]

Lovers must learn particular techniques and also learn to trust themselves and their partners. Our sexual moments can be highly spiritual, uniting the body, the lover, and God. Sex makes us particularly vulnerable to shame because it holds the power to lead us to ecstatic enlightenment or to devastating heartbreak. When sex is combined with abuse, all of its positives are distorted into a jumble of complicated negative emotions, influencing sexual functioning for years thereafter.

Remember earlier in the book when I said that guilt concludes, "I made a mistake," while shame says, "I am a mistake"? When we're in relationships we are bound to make mistakes, sometimes injuring feelings and damaging emotional connectedness. To restore relationships after damage has been done, feelings of guilt urge us toward forgiveness and repair. Regrets over sexual relationships are not as easily repaired, however, and frequently lead to shame. Because of strong taboos against talking about sex, we are more likely to be silent when sexual injuries occur, disrupting intimacy on many levels.

Sexual shame is so uniquely powerful that I give it a definition all its own. I define sexual shame as a feeling of unworthiness in the sight of God or significant others due to a sexual thought, desire, behavior, experience, or abuse. Sexual shame is a soul-defeating illness. It damages self-respect, intimate relationships between partners, and relationships among members in communities of faith. Sexual shame attacks people's self-worth to the point where they deem themselves unworthy of connection with anyone, including Jesus, God, Allah, Buddha, or any higher power. As different as we are from each other, we are all the same in this way. Our sexual thoughts, experiences, and behaviors have the potential to convince us that we are mercilessly unworthy of love. No other form of shame feels so private or drives us so deeply into hiding.[2]

WHERE THE SHAME BEGINS

We acquire varying amounts of sexual shame in childhood and adolescence. We catch it from the shame our parents or guardians carry. We catch it when our families keep sexual secrets. We catch it from perpetrators of sexual harassment or abuse who don't take responsibility for their actions and thereby pass the shame off onto their victims.

Like other forms of shame, sexual shame begins when we are young and vulnerable. It may start when as children we exhibited natural curiosity about our bodies, playfully joined another child to observe genitalia, or innocently explored touching with same-aged friends. A shocked and horrified parent who came upon such behavior may have conveyed the message that it is not okay by the look on his or her face, tone of voice, or condemning words. A connection is then established in our mind between sexual behaviors and shame. We may have learned to fear and hate our own bodies for getting us in trouble. Not knowing how to separate behavior from core self-worth, as children we simply conclude, "I'm dirty," "sick," or "bad."

In puberty we are particularly vulnerable to the onset of shame. Parents who make comments about our changing appearance, moods, and behaviors can unwittingly shame us. I remember coming into the living room at thirteen to show my father the new dress I was wearing. He muttered, "You look like a bean pole in that dress." At the exact time when I longed for curvy sexiness, these words stung like a slap in the face.

At puberty girls are given new rules about what to wear, how to sit, how much cleavage to reveal. Boys are shamed by parents for looking at sexual pictures online, in magazines, or in movies. Insensitive adults may comment at the dinner table on their developing teen's behaviors, including a daughter's moodiness during menstruation, a son's "wet dreams," and first crushes. It's a rare person who comes through adolescence unscathed.

As adolescents we learn the skill of social shaming and use it against each other, particularly in the sexual arena. Teens use sarcastic humor among peers, shaming anything out of the "ordinary." Boys experience a good deal of shame if their posture, gait, or voice is atypical. Inferences that they are "girls" or "fem" (implying homosexual) are used by bullies to heap massive doses of shame upon young men. It is common for adolescents to experience anxiety about gender roles and sexual identity. Ways these feelings are addressed in families make a marked difference between low levels of embarrassment and debilitating lifelong shame.

Overdoses of sexual shame negatively affect adolescent mental health. A teen in his or her first years of dating may try to avoid shame by obsessing about the sexual world in order to fit in. What if I'm too slow (or too fast) at it? What if I want it too much? What if my girlfriend shames me for trying to talk her into something? What if my boyfriend doesn't want me to have oral sex with him, and I won't do anything else? Anxiety and shame are gradually woven together in the developing persona. Without shame-less mentoring or parental acceptance, the teen has no one to help him or her place sandbags against this rising tide of shame.

To raise shame-less children and adolescents, parents need to lower their own anxiety about sexual thoughts, desires, and behaviors. So much has changed in the world of sexuality that parental lectures that begin with "When I was your age" are sure to be immediately dismissed. Parents need to affirm their sons and daughters when they express feelings of inadequacy or failure in their first infatuated love. They need to ask questions like, "What are you learning?" encouraging them to stay curious rather than get it right. Shame-less parents acknowledge the complexity of sexual development, offer education for protection against disease and pregnancy, set up negotiable guidelines for behavior, and allow for mistakes along the way.

Those who are lucky enough to have had shame-less adult help in getting through adolescence may yet bump into sexual shame in their older years while choosing a mate, engaging in preferred sexual behavior, and trying to communicate intense emotional reactions to sexual activities. When partnerships are formed and challenged by sexual dysfunctions or affairs, lowering shame is crucial to the maintenance of the relationship and for healing if the partnership ends.

When first sexual encounters are abusive, as they are for one in three girls and one in five boys, it can be hard to distinguish between love and hatred, pleasure and pain, or excitement and fear. Those who were sexually abused before adulthood by molestation, rape, or sexually laden verbal slander have a particularly tough time eradicating shame. When a sexual abuse survivor has sex with her husband, she sometimes has flashbacks to her incest.

A man who was forced to watch his sister being abused cannot have sex with any lights on. A woman whose soccer coach molested her as a teen has a hard time trusting partners and pushes them out of her life soon after she begins dating. A man whose father threw him out of the house for "acting like a queer" continues to struggle with questions about gender roles and sexual orientation. Multiple symptoms follow sexual abuse, including shame if pleasure was experienced during the abuse, and shame for not reporting it or stopping it.

Many good written resources are available for the healing of sexual abuse and for the partners of abuse victims. Having a partner who offers shame-free sexual exploration and who allows the abuse victim to guide the sexual encounter can greatly assist in the healing process. Sexual abuse victims need to talk about their experiences, and need nonthreatening sexual exchanges and the patient understanding of their partners. As sexual abuse victims move beyond the role of victim to being survivors, they relinquish shame during every step in the healing process.

Finding one's way to a shame-less sexual identity and ethical sexual behavior is a task worthy of everyone's attention and care. To lower shame it may be necessary to find a counselor, to tell an old secret, or to gain skill in conversations about sexual topics. An inventory of sexual experiences that still bring up shame is a good place to start, and once the list is made further exploration can take place. Why is this old experience still uncomfortable when I think about it? What could I do to get past this memory? How can I forgive myself for not stopping (or for initiating) an experience that harmed me or harmed someone else? Forgiveness can be applied to past behaviors, and then grace can begin to heal the shame.

The Influences of Previous Generations

Long before you explored sex for yourself, your ancestors connected a whole plethora of sexual activities with shame and reinforced those connections with religious teachings. A colleague at the San Francisco-based Institute for Advanced Study of Human Sexuality sent me a paper on which a label had been affixed. It said, "The most distributed 'sex ed' document ever by the Methodist Publishing house in Nashville."[3] The publication claimed to provide instruction and advice for young brides, written by a pastor's wife, Ruth Smythers, in 1894. Despite a lack of historic authenticity, it has been widely distributed, even used in a textbook at the university where I teach.[4] Its popularity lies in its satirical summary of the sexual mores of previous generations.

According to Ruth Smythers, it is the woman's job to tame her husband's libidinous passions and to keep the marriage from becoming "an orgy of sexual lust." The young bride is told to obey a cardinal rule in marriage, which is printed in capital letters: "GIVE LITTLE, GIVE SELDOM, AND ABOVE ALL, GIVE GRUDGINGLY." She is to deny him sex by "feigned illness, sleepiness and headaches," or "arguments, nagging, scolding, and bickering," which she says can be very effective "if used in the late evening about an hour before the husband would normally commence his seduction." She even suggests that on the wedding night the bride hopes that he will "stumble and incur some slight injury which she can use as an excuse to deny him sexual access." The woman must keep her husband on the proper path by making the sexual experience unpleasant. By their tenth anniversary, she says, "many wives have managed to complete their child bearing and have achieved the ultimate goal of terminating all sexual contacts with the husband."[5] In this worldview, the woman takes full responsibility for her own sexual behavior and that of her spouse.

Beliefs and attitudes like those reflected in Smythers's advice have their roots in patriarchal culture and ancient biblical principles that still influence sexual norms. Growing up surrounded by religious views on sexuality, you probably learned certain "rules" for sexual behavior—things like you shouldn't masturbate too much, and you should save yourself for marriage. Comedian and musician Butch Hancock also learned some rules. He said, "Life in Lubbock, Texas, taught me two things: One is that God loves you and you're going to burn in hell. The other is that sex is the

most awful, filthy thing on earth and you should save it for someone you love."[6] Maybe you learned some other rules that Butch
didn't mention, like not having sex with someone of your gender
or someone of a different race, ethnicity, or religion. In spite of
what you were being taught, if someone quoted the Bible to you,
you may have thought it was old and outdated. Maybe you threw
out your parents' or Sunday school teachers' rules without ever
knowing where they came from.

Those rules had been passed down from one generation to another for thousands of years to protect racial and religious blood-
lines. When God told Abraham (the father of Judaism, Islam, and
Christianity) that his descendants would number as the stars, quite
a few rules about sexuality were put in place to ensure this. People
were still in the dark about how pregnancy happens, and ancients
believed that the male's sperm contained everything necessary to
produce life. The woman contributed only a womb (the existence
and role of the egg was discovered later), so what happened with
male sperm mattered *a lot*. The sexual rules preserved sperm at
all costs. It would be a sin to waste it on anything other than its intended purpose, procreation. I call these "procreation-only" rules.

The procreation-only rules prohibited homosexuality, masturbation, and sex with another man's wife, which was also considered stealing the man's property. Sex was viewed as a blessing
when it reached its God-given goal of planting sperm in the womb
of a woman capable of childbearing. She could be a second or
third wife or a concubine. Whether she enjoyed sex or not was
entirely immaterial (though we now know that her orgasmic gyra-
tions actually provide motility for those little swimmers!). A man
did not need to have sex with an older wife, because she could no
longer have children, and it was expected that he would find a
younger wife or concubine and keep on producing offspring into
his older years. God must have winked at Abraham when he was
having sex with his postmenopausal wife Sarah, because the situation was entirely redeemed by her miraculous pregnancy!

These procreation-only rules were reinforced by male theologians, bishops, and clergy, many of whom had learned to fear

and despise their own and women's bodies as sources of sin, suffering, and shame. The rules gave men power over women's lives by limiting their spheres of influence, minimizing their contact with men, repeatedly forcing them into childbearing, and shaming them if no offspring were produced. Centuries later, various forms of these rules were still shaping people's beliefs, attitudes, and behaviors.

For plenty of our religious grandmothers, and some of our grandfathers, sex was an ordeal which had to be endured for the sake of procreation. All sexual activity was taboo except when performed in the dark with clothing on and with the intention to create offspring. The shame of all other (therefore *sinful*) sexual behavior has rested squarely on the shoulders of women. It's the woman's job to please her man, restrict his lust, and ensure that his seed always finds a proper repository in the womb of a virtuous Christian wife to whom he is bound in the covenant of marriage. If he has an affair, it is her fault; if he wants variety in the bedroom, she is too boring; if he masturbates, she isn't providing him with enough; if he watches pornography, she is obviously too prudish; if he leaves her for someone else, it resulted from her insufficiency. These shame-filled and false presumptions are the lingering aftermath of gender-biased ideologies. They presume that men cannot control their own sexual fantasies and behaviors, leading to the idea that "boys will be boys" and excuses such as, "He just couldn't help himself."

These old ideas about sex, the weakness of men, and women's responsibility for enforcing proper sexual behavior still exist within the dominant culture. The idea that men are not responsible for their sexual arousal or behavior is used to reinforce gender roles in the family. Women are still saddled with the job of protecting themselves, their husbands, and their children from sexual lust and its associated shame. In my community a congregation holds classes instructing engaged women on these responsibilities. They are given Bible verses teaching them to submit to their husband's sexual passions so that he will not stray into pornography or affairs during the marriage. They are given the moral duty to engage in sexual intercourse whenever he requests or demands it, in order to reign in his tendency toward lasciviousness. When these duties are not fulfilled, the woman is shamed by her partner and her religious community.

Procreation-only rules have wide-ranging implications. The combination of religious legalisms, gender rigidity, and cultural stigma intensify women's experiences of shame. Courtship rituals under strict supervision, the practice of suturing women's labia to ensure virginal purity, and arranged marriages all intend to protect women from social rejection and economic hardship without a suitable mate. Debates over abortion rights and restrictions are often about the power of the woman to make decisions about her body and frequently induce shame. They include shame for women's "failure" to use appropriate protection, shame about her economic status, and shame for her decision to put her life before the life of "her" fetus. Men are not shamed in this way, partially from the procreation-only ethic, which suggests that they have appropriately created offspring. Again, we see ways that sexual shame is handed out differently depending on gender.

Many people are not aware of the role that millennia-old rules still play in our society. Sometimes at workshops I playfully ask the participants to raise their hands if they have broken the procreation-only rules that I describe. It takes them awhile to think that out. Keeping the rules means they have never masturbated, they have never used birth control, they have avoided all sex during menstruation, and they have discontinued (or expect to end) sexual relations after menopause. One at a time, nearly all of their hands go up. Everyone laughs as the irony becomes clear. We are acting as if we have well spelled-out rules for what's okay and what isn't, but people of faith are just as confused about them as people in the broader culture. In the absence of a well thought-out ethic on sexual behavior, we are left with fragments of old rules that are difficult to apply. Most congregations and clergy preach that these rules are still definitive and operative.

EDUCATION ON THE WAY TO
BECOMING SHAME-LESS

Many important scholars and researchers in the field of sexuality have helped to loosen the grip of shame from outdated morality codes. No one pushed the culture faster or further out of its Victorian perspectives than human sexuality researcher Alfred Kinsey (1894–1956). Having been strictly taught about sexual "sin," he became a powerful voice for grace when facts were needed to correct fictions. I have been curious about his life and work since finding a copy of one of his books on a shelf in my father's den nearly forty years ago.

The biographical film *Kinsey* depicts the life's work of Alfred Kinsey.[7] In an opening scene, we find an adolescent Alfred and a younger friend in their scout uniforms at the side of a lake on a sunny day. Alfred had been taught by his father (a Methodist preacher) to loath sexuality and to view it as a tool of the devil. His nocturnal erections created intense shame for him. The younger friend, who was having a similar problem, tells Al, "I had one of those old fits again . . . I tried to stop it." Alfred takes out his Bible and suggests that they read the Scriptures and pray. The two of them, with pained expressions on their upturned faces, kneel by the lake and pray, but we are left to guess the wording of their guilty confessions and pleas for forgiveness. Over time Alfred Kinsey recognized and publically proclaimed that sexual impulses are not, in and of themselves, wrong or immoral.

Kinsey had a bright and curious mind about all living species, so he became a biologist and studied the reproductive patterns of gall wasps. He did not foresee that he would become famous instead for his groundbreaking research in the field of human sexuality. Kinsey's personal rebellion against his father, and the religious culture in which he had learned to be ashamed, took the form of fact-finding research that overturned prevailing myths about masturbation, sexual orientation, premarital sexuality, sexual frequency, and sexual techniques. By anonymously interviewing thousands of subjects, he was able to replace myth with fact. He lifted the repression of moralistic religious teaching and taboos. In searching for the truth about human sexual behavior, he relocated the discussion of sexuality from pulpit harangue to academic research.

Thirty years after Kinsey's first book, *Sexual Behavior in the Human Male*,[8] had been published, I was a curious adolescent. I went through the house looking for reading material so that I could learn more about sexuality. All we had in the house at that time was a few *National Geographic* magazines with pictures of remote societies around the world—including those where children and adults wore little or no clothing. We also had a very large, hardbound copy of Kinsey's 1948 book, which was later referred to as the *The Kinsey Report*. It was dull reading, with statistical tables I was not able to interpret. Why did we have a copy of this book? I went off to college with my curiosity and found a good deal of information there. But, like the students at Kinsey's university, my sexuality education was based on rumor and innuendo, locker room talk and late-night chats in the dorm. After college I was further educated in the seminary environment where, frankly, the sexual boundaries were even less rigid than they had been at my Christian college. Faculty had sexual flings with students without reprimand, students swapped partners, and sexual experimentation was commonplace throughout the nine multidenominational seminaries on our campus. We can say that this was just the seventies, but I hear graduates across several decades talking about similar seminary experiences. While deans and presidents willingly overlooked sexual behaviors, they also overlooked sexual coercion and the misuse of power. Recent advances have been made in the development of policies on sexual harassment and sexual ethics at seminaries, but policies don't provide education or conversations about the nuances of sexuality and professional conduct.[9] Most clergy have not had classes in human sexuality, and I doubt that Kinsey's books are found in many seminary libraries.

Ten years after I graduated from seminary both of my parents died within a two-year span. I went home to sort out the family belongings and to learn more about home as a place in the heart as well as a place you once lived. Still twenty years from earning my PhD in psychology, I nonetheless went quickly to Dad's book-shelf, where for many years, Kinsey's groundbreaking book had been stuffed among photo albums, how-to books, and old Bibles handed down by our grandparents. The book was missing.

Why did I even care to find an outdated work with question-able research methodology and controversial findings? I pre-sumed by then that my gay father read this book in his search to become free of shame. Kinsey was among the first researchers to publically recognize the diversity of sexual orientations and to claim their normalcy. In a 1948 letter to a concerned correspon-dent, Kinsey wrote, "One of the worst things that can happen to a person is to have them feel that they are abnormal or different from other persons."[10] His work was described by *Harper Magazine* as "a plea for greater tolerance," and the reporter noted, "Such terms as abnormal, unnatural, oversexed and undersexed, have little validity in light of Professor Kinsey's revelations."[11] The rev-elations themselves (particularly his data on the wide range of sexual orientations and behaviors) were astonishing at the time and challenged the pervasive oppression of sexual shame in the culture. We in the fields of psychology, research, and theology owe him a debt of gratitude.

SHAME AND THE CHANGING CULTURE

Nothing more earthshaking than Kinsey's research occurred in the field of human sexuality until advances in contraception were made nearly two decades later. The women's liberation move-ment and the introduction of "the pill" radically changed the landscape of sexual behavior for women and men in the 1970s and '80s. As it became possible for women to engage in non-procreative sexual activity without fearing the consequence of pregnancy and as safer abortions were made available, men and women became more equal partners in decision making about their relationships. Women were less beholden to men in their choices about sexual behavior and its consequences and less likely to live within the constrictions of their grandmothers' shame-bound rules. Patriarchal norms of proper and improper sexual behavior lost their power.

Once women and men could protect against unwanted pregnancy, they could approach their sexual lives with less anxiety and move toward experimentation. Betty Dodson, PhD, a sexuality educator, began teaching women to study their own bodies and their sexual responses so that they could become better sexual partners and experience the pleasure of sexuality that men had been enjoying for centuries. Her book *Sex for One,* published in 1974, is still popular and helpful to women who have never experienced the sexual responses of their own bodies.[12] Another significant resource, *Our Bodies, Ourselves,* published in 1976, provided women with medical and sexual information.[13] *The Joy of Sex,* first published in 1972, introduced readers to drawings of various sexual positions and reached people who would never have looked at pictures like those in any other source due to taboos about pornography.[14]

Over the next thirty years, the explosion of the Internet, social networking sites, and text messaging took sex public. Once home-computer users could access pictures and videos right from their desks, sexually explicit sites became abundant. Late-night television shows provided education, as Dr. Drew and Dr. Ruth answered questions about sexual problems, and sitcoms such as *Frasier* and *Friends* frequently talked about sex. By the time *Sex in the City* taught the TV audience how to use vibrators, the prevalence of educational materials about sex was widespread. Nearly three decades after the introduction of the birth control pill, a student introduced me to the book *Cunt,*[15] written by a young woman who dared to take the power out of the word *cunt,* transforming shame into power and acceptance. You can imagine the look on the face of the clerk in the bookstore when I ordered my copy and said the title out loud! The book takes a fresh look at the use of slang to denigrate women's bodies and ways to take the sting out of those words. It also illustrates how conversations about sex have evolved in the past few decades.

Gender-biased sexual shame is less tolerated than ever before. In 2011 a police officer in Toronto told a group of coeds at York University's Osgoode Hall Law School that to prevent rape, they shouldn't dress like sluts.[16] This comment implies that victims of sexual assault are responsible for their attacker's behavior. While the beauty industry spends billions of dollars per year marketing clothing, makeup, and hair products to increase women's sex appeal, women are then blamed for arousing men by their seductive appearance. They are blamed for unsolicited sexual advances and even violence against them. She "egged him on," she "came on to him," she dressed "provocatively," she "ran with a bad crowd," are examples of shame-based comments made about women who are harmed by harassment, abuse, and rape. Having internalized these ideas prevalent in the wider culture, it is not surprising that assault victims are reluctant to come forward about abuse. When this incident occurred in Toronto, a group of women decided to use their power to turn shame into pride. They organized a "slut walk" on the streets in Toronto, with subsequent walks in Boston and other cities in North America. These marches were specifically designed to educate communities on ways to stop shaming victims of violence.

Pioneers like Kinsey, Dodson, Westheimer, Muscio, and women marching on city streets have found ways to take the shame out of sex. For the most part, they have rejected sexual biases inherent in most religious traditions. They have moved the culture toward a greater tolerance of diversity and gender equality. Sexuality has been moved out of the private realm and become a topic of public discourse. Now that explicit materials are readily available to all ages via the Internet, and social networks allow for sexualized conversations around the clock, procreation-only ethics have become outdated and irrelevant.

Does religion influence sexuality at all in the current culture? Could it? Is something lacking in the dominant culture's presentation of sexuality that could be helped by religious influences? Do the synagogue and church have anything to learn about sexuality from the world beyond their sanctuaries? In the next chapter I will turn to these questions and address issues of sexual shame in congregations.

CHAPTER 9

Sexual Shame in Congregations
Old Habits and New Opportunities

When sexuality becomes puzzling or painful to us, and as it changes across the lifespan, we need shame-less places in which to tell our stories, ask questions, and find answers. Could your congregation become such a place? Let me describe a few scenes from sexually shame-less congregations.

A small multiethnic group of women and a few men gather in a comfortable meeting room and talk about sexual violence. Their congregation makes healing sexual abuse a mission priority, and they get together every week to read *Getting Well Again*, a book for abuse survivors.[1] They share their stories of abuse, they pray for one another, and because they have a shame-less leader, they receive grace to help them overcome their fear, pain, and self-hatred.

In another congregation a young adult stands at a white board leading a forum in which parents and teens are gathered to talk about sex. He says, "When you love yourself, you love God, and you love your partner with equal respect, then sex is awesome." I can picture the teens blushing and giggling. "Remember," he continues, "your body is the temple of God, which is a big responsibility. In this class you'll learn how to protect your bodies and to protect the body of your partners if you make the choice to exchange body fluids in any way." I can see curious parents who are relieved to learn some things they didn't know about keeping their kids safe. The class includes tips on cybersex predators, preventing date rape, sexual addiction, and other sex practices that are particularly dangerous.

Behind the towering old stone façade of a downtown church, a group of people in their middle years are at a meeting of the education committee, opening boxes and looking at the new Sunday school curriculum for children of all ages on staying safe, strong, and abuse free.[2] On Sunday morning stately mahogany pews are full and people are laughing together as the pastor preaches from the Song of Songs and affirms the goodness of sensual and erotic love.

At a synagogue on the outskirts of the city, couples go to a class where they talk about what makes sex sacred (or not) and how to be more attuned to each other when they are intimate. They learn how to talk with each other before, during, and after sex. They recall the absurdly shame-infused lessons they were taught by their parents and their first bumbling awkward sexual experiences. They gain confidence about being imperfect yet mature lovers.

A Bible study group meets on the sprawling campus of a rapidly growing church that attracts members from several nearby counties. They study sections of the Scriptures where harassment, incest, and rape occur and openly talk about ways to work for justice to end incest and other sexual trauma. A man describes his salvation as God leading him through recovery from sexual abuse. A woman tells a tearful story of the Holy Spirit guiding her counselor to help her so that she could let go of her fear. This congregation's commitment to justice includes keeping its own members free of harassment and abuse. Every member is given a copy of their sexual harassment and abuse policies, and every new member receives education during the new members' class on ways to spot, stop, and report abuse.

Gay, lesbian, bisexual, transgendered, and questioning (GLBTQ) members and their families aren't singled out at a sexually shame-less congregation in a small Midwest town. Sexual minorities are simply part of the family. Diverse partnerships are affirmed and blessed at the altar. The congregation offers support groups for the children of GLBTQ parents and the parents of GLBTQ children so that they can deal with the stigma of being a so-called different family, harassment by the dominant culture, and the indignities their loved ones suffer at the hands of believers and nonbelievers alike.

In a sexually shame-less congregation next door to a college, a mission study group discusses the overlapping dynamics of sexuality, gender, and racial prejudice. Congregants plan programs to confront injustice in their communities, assist domestic abuse survivors, and provide students with rape-prevention information. They work with community leaders to ensure that racial and sexual minorities are represented in rape-crisis-response teams and services for abuse survivors. They send letters to newspaper editors addressing racial prejudice when it is couched in sexual stereotyping. They invite speakers from diverse communities to teach them more about the global epidemics of child abuse, sex trafficking, prostitution, and the use of sexual violence as genocide.

In my idealistic vision of these congregations, any subject of sexuality that is puzzling, painful, or disruptive to relationships can be discussed, and help can be found. Paul also had a vision of the church in which everyone's needs would be met. "With great power the apostles gave their testimony to the resurrection of the Lord Jesus, and great grace was upon them all" (Acts 4:33). We can make healing shame and offering grace our highest priority for individuals within and beyond our sanctuaries. We can join the dominant culture's discourse on sexuality once again, and do so shame-lessly.

Mistakes We Need to Confess and Correct

Although I have a clear image of the sexually healthy congregation, I recognize that it will take a great deal of grace and courage to move in this direction. Congregation leaders are up against some powerful forces. Beyond our sanctuary walls, fireside rooms, social halls, and school classrooms, congregants live in an entirely different world when it comes to sexuality.

Sexuality in the dominant culture has become entangled with marketing and manipulation. Our consumer culture markets sex as a commodity. If commercials can make you anxious about sexual performance, you're more likely to buy products and pharmaceuticals. If they arouse you, you are more likely to buy their blue jeans and sports cars. Consumer sex says that you should keep up with your neighbors who are doing it more than you are, and that pleasure is the goal *above all else*. Consumer sex is vacuous and exploitative.

The prevalence of pornography, sexualized media, and unbridled sexual behavior in our culture leads to this implied motto: "You can have all of the sex you want without repercussions." This lie flies in the face of sexual dangers such as sexually transmitted infections and responsibility for pregnancy. It also leaves out the mental and spiritual components of sexual behavior. It is disinterested in matters of the heart, the psyche, and the soul. Consumer sex is performance driven, with orgasmic pleasure as its goal. It pays no attention at all to negative consequences that could arise during or after sexual exchanges. It couldn't care less about love or intimacy.

It's no wonder that when adolescents and young adults are influenced by the fantasy of consequence-free sexuality, they disconnect from their faith traditions. They think that religious ideas about sex are narrow and outdated. Most teens begin accessing pornography on the Internet during adolescence.[3] The age of first intercourse is around seventeen years and has declined in the last decade, but according to a Kaiser Family Foundation study, a third of sexually active teens reported "being in a relationship where they felt things were moving too fast sexually," and one-fourth of them had "done something sexual they didn't really want to do."[4] In a self-report study of high school students, between 8 and 12 percent of them reported sexual contact with same-gendered partners.[5] In their college years the majority of students are engaging in sex to screen out (or in) potential long-term partners, while others have "friends with benefits," partners with whom they never intend to have an emotional or lasting relationship. When the experimentation is over, when young adults sigh, "Been there, done that," they are still, like all of us, yearning for loving connection. They may not be able to articulate it in the language of faith, with words like sacred or holy or spiritual, but they long for something more. They long for sexuality with less anxiety and more intimacy.

Congregation leaders have attempted to counter cultural messages about sexuality, but often with destructive results. A popular pastor in a huge congregation decided to assist his flock in becoming more sex positive. He preached a sermon on sexual intimacy in marriage, and then assigned husbands and wives to have sex with each other every day for a week.[6] When I described this sermon to a group of friends, one who had been in a sexually abusive marriage, she said, "Oh great, some of those women will be raped this week." While this was a startling statement, on reflection I believe she is right. Some of the women and men in these marriages may be forced or obliged to have sex rather than participate with a willing spirit. When people are forced into sexual activities they are not prepared for, sex can be painful emotionally and physically. Rape takes place in many partnerships and is more likely in heterosexual marriages when men believe that the Bible says they have the authority and a God-given right to dictate their wives' compliance. Mandated sexual behavior is not healthy and does not foster marital intimacy, advance gender equality, or cure shame.

In another effort to deal with culturally dominant views on sexuality, some preachers and congregations take steps to reinforce the "no sex before marriage" rule with teens, increasing teens' anxiety during this sensitive developmental stage. Teen girls pledge to their fathers to remain virgins until marriage. Sometimes their fathers give them a promise ring during an elaborate ritual. The girl's fear of disappointing others and her desire to avoid public shame supposedly reinforces her behavior. Studies have shown that those girls do not, in fact, remain virgins longer than their peers and that they are less likely to use protection during sexual behavior. They are also more likely than nonpledging teen cohorts to carry lingering guilt about their behavior.[7] This strategy turns out to be a misguided attempt to enforce the sacredness of sexuality, but because it increases shame, it leaves young women ill-prepared for sexual intimacy. What they need is candid and complete education about sexuality as a physical, psychological, *and* spiritual activity, one with consequences in all three areas, as well.

Addressing Past Abuse

I'm not surprised that people don't look to their congregations for sexuality education. Only when religious professionals clean up their own act about harassment and professional misconduct will they regain the trust of young people within and outside our faith communities. Sexually shame-less congregations become proactive about naming and correcting abuses within their congregations and denominations. If we don't address the damage of sexual-abuse shame, our congregations will continue to be diseased and will decline. I firmly believe that sexual legalisms, denial about abuse, and shame-blame games contribute to the inevitable closure of many congregations.

While the dangers of sexual sin have been continually preached, clergy and lay leaders have been crossing sexual boundaries within their congregations with few consequences. Roughly one in three congregations has been harmed by sexual abuse. Places of healing have instead become places of wounding for many victims of molestation, harassment, and sexual assault. While most sexual misconduct that is revealed has been by clergy, new statistics point to the enormous amount of sexual abuse by laity toward both other members and their clergy. In anonymous surveys, more than one-third of people who attend worship say they have experienced sexual harassment at church. Nearly three-fourths of clergy report harassment by laity.[8] These statistics point to the overwhelming prevalence of a previously unmentionable problem. They bring us out of complacency and denial while challenging us to keep up our efforts to abuse-proof congregations.

Worsening the situation, clergy at every level, from bishops to collegial support groups, have attempted to avoid shame by playing the blame-shame game. They have fostered secrecy by claiming that records about clergy sexual abuse are protected by the supervisory mandate of confidentiality. Clergy who offend are often removed without explanation and relocated to congregations where members are not informed of the clergyperson's history. While attempting to minimize the shame of public exposure, congregational leaders and denominational leaders have harmed victims. Sometimes their silence is tragically exchanged for remuneration in a court of law.

A survivor of clergy sexual abuse told her judicatory leaders about repeated incidents of abuse. The credibility of her testimony was fully acknowledged in the privacy of the conference office, but when the bishop sent a letter to all of the congregations in his jurisdiction to report the defrocking of the offending clergyperson, it said simply that he had engaged in "misconduct" of a sexual nature. For the victim, who had been molested and repeatedly forced into sexual activity with her pastor when she was an under-aged teen, this level of minimization was painfully insulting. In any other circumstance, the pastor's behavior would have been called pedophilia or child rape. To avoid shaming the perpetrator or the church as an institution, the denomination ended up heaping greater shame upon the victim.[9]

Victims need to be heard, believed, and provided with counseling. Victims need to be consulted and given as much consideration as are the opinions of lawyers who are consulted. Victims need genuine apologies and financial compensation for therapy, and they need to be respected as teachers in prevention and healing. In one case, the victim asked the judicatory to create an abuse prevention Sunday and to provide classes and resources on abuse prevention for children and adolescents. These are steps that victims are taking to free their denominations and congregations from further abuse and the shame that binds them.

Victims, survivors, and their supporters face an uphill climb in their efforts to hold the church accountable for its missteps. Leaders in most denominations over the past few decades will

we think shame will
keep people away.

confess privately that they "lost files" and relocated boundary-violating clergy, all to cover up abuses. When I tell people that I provide abuse-prevention workshops in Protestant churches, people often say, "Oh, I thought that was just a Catholic problem." Daily headlines report abuses of power in the form of sexual harassment and sexual abuse by clergy across denominations and at all levels.

ENDING THE SHAME-BLAME DYNAMIC

Most denominations have become astute at playing the shame-blame game. An example of this arose when the Roman Catholic United States Conference of Bishops commissioned a study of underlying causes for abuse by the John Jay College of Criminal Justice at the City University of New York.[10] The study pointed to the cultural permissiveness of the 1960s and '70s as a root cause of abuse by Catholic priests. Victim advocacy organizations seized upon this presumption as a form of the shame-blame game, wherein the bishops blame the popular culture, rather than placing responsibility on the perpetrators and secrets kept by denominational leaders. Jim FitzGerald from Call to Action, an organization of Catholics who support the inclusion of sexual minorities in the life of the church, said this of the report: "It is equally possible that those upheavals [of the 1960s and '70s] which gave people new courage to oppose repressive authoritarian structures, made it more possible for abused Catholics who had long been carrying heavy secrets to come forward."[11] Those who attempt to confront church leaders about abuse and systemic dynamics that perpetuate it must name and stop the use of blame as a diversion for the underlying shame experienced within the denomination. Those seeking reform can expect these conversations to be difficult.

Once denominational leaders have lost integrity, authority, and respect with their constituents, it's hard for them to regain authority. To address the issue of sexual shame in the church, more leaders need to come forward and name these subtle shifts in blame for what they are—attempts to avoid responsibility and the shame that arises along with it. Only by admitting that they have been secretive in order to avoid shame will denominational leaders regain a trusted place at the discussion table. Making training a funding priority, reaching out to current and former victims, and establishing no-tolerance policies with consequences for offending clergy and laity will increase trust. As more congregants demand shame-less and ethical approaches to the problem of sexual abuse, changes will slowly take place.

Denominational executives, congregations, and clergy who must deal with the aftermath of mishandled abuse cases feel overburdened by the enormity of the task. Over a holiday a friend of mine brought me sourdough starter in a jar with holes punched in the lid. I'm thinking, "Now what am I going to do with that?" It's rather foul smelling and emits gasses in my refrigerator. Every week I have to tend to it, stirring it, dumping out half of it (or cooking with it), and adding more flour and water. I know it makes delicious pancakes, because he made them for us on the visit. I hear it makes great breads and biscuits. But it needs a lot of care that I'm not sure I'm up for. Meanwhile, the starter sits in my refrigerator and stinks.

The reluctance I feel in dealing with the sourdough starter is the way clergy and congregations understandably respond when their resources, time, and mission are diverted into policies, conversations, task forces, training programs, and lawsuits in the aftermath of abuse. Denominational leaders can no longer avoid the task of abuse prevention and healing, however, because the numbers of incidents of harassment keep growing and become foul when nothing is done to stop them. As denominational leaders acknowledge their complicity and change their practices, congregational leaders must also acknowledge shame and end the blame. Shame may be terribly uncomfortable, but blame provides only temporary relief. In the end, blame leaves individuals and congregations feeling powerless and incapable of change.

To overcome the shame, congregations and clergy need to proactively address sexuality issues across the lifespan, increasing the congregation's comfort level with sexual subjects. They need to talk more frequently about healthy sexuality as well as its distortions and dangers. Then, when sexual abuse surfaces from present or past behaviors, they can facilitate conversations with a great deal less fear and anxiety.

Another version of the shame-blame game is played out as congregations and denominations focus enormous amounts of energy and anxiety on legislation regulating the participation of sexual minorities. Rather than face the enormous shame of sexual behaviors such as clergy abuse, laity harassment, adultery, pornography, and other sexual issues for congregants, the shame is placed on one small segment of the population. In the past several decades congregational leaders and clergy have been in pitched battles over what is called the "issue of homosexuality," which is often a debate about biblical inerrancy and an attempt to hold on to ancient purity codes. The fight for full inclusion has been going on for several decades with no signs of slowing down.

Because people in the broader culture are generally more accepting of sexual diversity, they just shake their heads and sigh over these pitched battles in congregations and choose not to participate in faith communities. The focus on homosexuality is way out of proportion. As if this were the only issue to be discussed! If nine of ten congregants self-define as "straight," what is being said of *their* sexuality? How are congregations helping people of all sexual orientations address sexual shame for wanting it more or less, for growing up with abuse, for engaging in "promiscuity," for faking orgasms, for enjoying erotica or pornography, for addictive sexual behaviors, for objectifying their own bodies or the bodies of others, for the fact that even when they have sexual encounters they feel disconnected, distant, and lonely.

Who is helping people with these sexual behaviors and their sexual emptiness or shame? As people find themselves surrounded by sexual images, jokes, and erotica, where can they turn? Could you see it as your job, as a leader in a faith community, to educate people about spiritual and ethical sexuality? Congregants watch hundreds of sexual scenes on their televisions every week, their families all have a gay or lesbian member somewhere on the family tree, they have experienced marriages torn apart after affairs, and some of them struggle with a sexual addiction. It is time for congregations to provide forums where *all* of these issues are discussed.

Sadly, faith communities have even avoided conversations about the spiritual aspects of sexuality, although spirituality is *supposed to be* their forte. It is a rare parish, congregation, or synagogue that helps people to understand and experience their sexuality as sacred, their intimacy as communion with God and with one another. Ironically, faith communities are uniquely positioned to assist congregants and constituents in finding the connection between the sacred and sexuality. Except for their shame, I believe they would already be doing this. To lower the shame, and to bring spiritual values into the conversation, let's engage in conversations about sexual ethics.

SHAME-LESS SEXUAL ETHICS

To turn our focus toward sacred sexuality, I suggest that individuals and congregations engage in conversations about ethical sexual behavior. For more than a decade now, I've been helping people both within and outside the church describe their own sexual boundaries and define them clearly. Recognizing that what popular culture describes as ideal and what the church or synagogue has long defined as ideal may not reflect an individual's actual values and beliefs.

Each semester, in the university class I teach, I give students the opportunity to obtain extra credit by completing a handout in which they write out a sexual ethic for themselves. When I ask them to describe the influence that religion plays on their sexual decisions, the majority of them say that they have left prior influences behind and no longer live within the boundaries of any religious teaching. Most students are puzzled by the idea that religion has anything relevant to say about their sexuality. They have rejected the legalisms of their parents' faith traditions, but some of them have not given much thought to the values that influence their day-to-day sexual decision making. By developing a sexual ethic, they come away with less anxiety and more confidence about their sexuality. They move from "just say yes" or "just say no" to a more complex ethical approach in which principles guide behavior.

A copy of a worksheet on developing a sexual ethic has been provided in appendix A. Clergy can use this for themselves and help their members develop sexual ethics too. The worksheet can be reproduced as long as the copyright notice appears on all copies. Please use this document as a starting place for dialogue.

To foster even greater awareness, I have provided a second appendix called "When Sex Moves Out of Bounds." It lists psychological dangers, physical dangers, relational dangers, and congregational dangers regarding sexuality. Resist any temptation to use it as a list of rules. Instead, use it as a resource to deepen conversations about sexual ethics that make real sense in today's world. Sound intimidating? You could ask a sexuality educator from your community to assist you in guiding participants through this process. We all need safe places to dialogue about ethical and unethical sexual behavior and to connect our religious beliefs with our actual sexual practices.

What issues might arise in completing these questionnaires? Participants might confess problems that they have long ignored or been too ashamed to talk about. Some dominant themes would include the use of computer pornography, sexual harassment in the workplace, and depression affecting sexual interest. It is essential that leaders of groups who begin these conversations be shame-less in their approaches to all concerns and that they be able to listen to people's stories without judgment. A trained counselor or health-care professional can often safely guide these discussions. Most sexual behaviors that individuals engage in serve a purpose for them—enabling them to experience pleasure, overcome shame, become closer to someone. Like other aspects of our lives, sexuality is usually enlisted for something good, right, or corrective within the personality and relationship. No single behavior is always right (righteous) or always wrong (sinful).

Before you lead a discussion of sexual ethics, please reread the section of this book on how and why to avoid calling anyone a sinner (beginning on page 25). Shame is lifted when people learn that they are not as damaged as they once believed themselves to be. Their sexual history or current struggles with sexuality need not separate them from the love of God. Everyone struggles with some aspect of their sexual past, and grace-filled conversations allow them to end years of soul-defeating shame.

WHEN CLERGY HAVE LINGERING SHAME

For clergy to help their congregants lower shame and live sexually healthy lives, they must be sexually healthy themselves. According to Debra W. Haffner, a sexuality educator for congregations, sexually healthy religious professionals "are comfortable with their own sexuality, have the skills to provide pastoral care and worship on sexuality issues, and are committed to sexual justice in the congregation and the society at large."[12] A self-assessment for religious professionals is available in her resource on creating sexually healthy faith communities. While many clergy aspire to meet these characteristics, many have unhealed sexual shame that blocks their ability to achieve these goals.

Congregations and denominations are limited in their ability to screen for sexually healthy or sexually damaged individuals when hiring religious professionals. Most clergy candidates are given psychological evaluations before or during seminary education, but they are rarely asked for sexual histories by interviewing psychologists. This is particularly true in denominations where clergy who acknowledge homosexuality are denied ordination. When sexual histories are not explored, congregations may not know if their candidates are able to keep sexual boundaries in professional relationships, are able to live within required covenants of fidelity, or have tendencies toward addictive behaviors, which could include pornography and sexual predation. Thorough evaluation and training for clergy during candidacy is essential. Candidates need to understand the restrictions upon them for dating and sexual behavior both within and beyond congregations. They need safe places within their denominations to discuss ways to meet or sublimate their sexual needs as required by denominational policies.

A single clergywoman in her midforties had just finished seminary and was hired as pastor of a rural church. She knew that she had the eyes of the community upon her. When she began dating a man from a different area, she was conflicted. In the dominant culture outside the congregation, most people would have thought it normal for a midlife female to travel and stay overnight with a man she was dating or for him to travel and stay with her. They would not have been concerned about whether the overnight included sexual behavior. But she, like most single clergy, had agreed at her ordination to be celibate. She decided to take her dilemma to the personnel committee of her congregation, which was amazingly courageous of her. She asked what they thought about his staying at the parsonage when he was in town and how they thought this would be handled by the rest of the congregation. They were supportive and said, "It's none of our business, is it?" According to the policies of her denomination, they could have fired her or brought charges against her if they suspected her of having a sexual relationship prior to marriage. In this case, they simply encouraged her to live a free and happy life, chose to respect her privacy with regard to sexual choices she might make, and told her that they would defend her against the protests of instrusive parishioners.

She had clearly gone before a grace-filled group of leaders in a shame-less congregation. Yet their agreement may not have ended her own struggle with shame, because she was caught between two loyalties. A painful reality for single clergy and for homosexual, bisexual, and transgendered clergy is that many of them have denominational restrictions on sexual behavior that force them either to forego sexual relationships or to live in disobedience to the covenants they agree to at ordination. While some rare congregations may support a pastor or rabbi who is dating, sexually active single clergy know the risk that someone could bring charges against them. This forces some of them into marriages prematurely. Others, who do not have the option of marriage because of their sexual orientation, live in the painful tension between enjoying an open, loving partnership at the risk of defrocking or living with vigilant secrecy. Keeping secrets about one's sexual and relational life is heartbreaking and shame producing. Let's admit it: "Don't ask, don't tell," simply "don't" work. It increases shame among sexual minorities and does nothing to address the breaking of covenants by clergy who engage in sexual abuse or infidelity. I have long been dismayed by the inequity in the ways that rules against various sexual behaviors are ignored or enforced.

Clergy have plenty of their own unresolved feelings about sexual behaviors, attractions, or abuses, and therefore, just like everyone else, they fear the rising shame and blame that conversations about such issues trigger. To be shame-less while discussing sexual topics, ministry professionals need to have reviewed their own sexual histories and addressed areas of pain and guilt in therapy or under supervision. Unresolved sexual problems will be transferred to current relationships, explicitly sexual or not, for good or ill. My plea to clergy is that they be diligent in reducing their own shame. Then they can establish coherent sexual ethics that protect them and their congregations, become role models and teachers for spiritually imbued sexuality, and create environments of grace.

ADDITIONAL STARTING PLACES

Congregations can have an enormous influence on the development of sexual attitudes and behaviors among children and youth. It's time for congregations to join parents and school systems as sexuality educators. Today's preadolescents are as curious about sexuality as I was when I searched my family home for books with pictures and details about sex. None of us need to begin our sexual lives with shame heaped upon us, but most of us need education and acceptance in order to feel joy and pride. Across the lifespan, we all want to feel those sexual urges and say, "I praise you, [God], for I am fearfully and wonderfully made" (Ps. 139:14).

My thought at this point is that you, dear reader, may still be wishing it was *somebody else's* job to educate congregants about sexuality. The problem is that nobody else is doing the job, at least not doing it within a framework of faith-based values and ethics. Schools provide education about reproduction but not about ethical decision making. Parents are still pretty frightened while talking with their kids about it. Conversations about the sacredness of sexuality, the ways it both fosters bonding and can wreck the soul need to take place in faith communities. Becoming shame-less entails casting off antiquated and overly legalistic approaches, honoring diversity, keeping a spirit of playfulness about the ordinary folly of love and sex, and claiming ourselves and others as worthy of God's embrace, regardless of the damage we have suffered through our sexual experiences. Remember, the unique contribution of people of faith is our ability to heal shame with grace.

Who is going to teach that gospel, that good news to the children, preadolescents, and adolescents who encounter repeated sexual content in the media and among their peers? They need a whole lot more guidance than being handed a Bible and told to pray about it, as young Kinsey advised when he was on the banks of the river with his friend. They need to understand the connection between their spirituality and sexuality and to understand positive self-esteem and the debilitating damage of shame. If congregations don't assist them or provide training for parents to assist them, then the Internet will, providing them with a whole different message. They'll go looking for facts and find pictures or learn about things to do that you and I have never even considered in our fantasies. What they will find on the Web is skewed pictures of what sexual partners in real life do together, pictures that shock them while tempting them to experiment in ways that may be unrealistic and dangerous.

For example, a young man watching porn stars in sexual situations might become anxious that his penis isn't the right size. He needs to hear the good news that his body is okay just as it is, that he can give and receive love without "perfect" body parts. Perhaps by watching videos of violent sex, he could come to believe that women want to be raped. He needs to hear, instead, that respect and equality are values worth holding on to, and that violence is never okay. A young woman might believe that providing oral sex for her boyfriend does not involve any risks, not knowing the dangers of the transmission of sexually transmitted infections (STIs). She needs someone to tell her the facts about diseases and that she risks her self-esteem, her sense of sacred worth, and her physical health when she engages in some sexual behaviors. Who among us will have the training and courage to shame-lessly talk with these young people? It's time for every participant in every congregation to become fearless in approaching sexual subjects and for clergy and leaders to embrace this urgent call to ministry.

Clergy and lay leaders in congregations in which most members are older may conclude that sexuality isn't relevant to the population they serve. Nothing could be farther from the truth. As older congregants face changes in their sexual lives they experience increased marital stress, pain and loss due to aging or illness, and lowered self-esteem. They need places to safely discuss the changes within their relationship due to menopause or erectile dysfunction. Many of them have never heard that sacred sexuality can be even more pleasurable when it is no longer goal driven. The shift from a focus on orgasmic sexual behavior to enhancing intimacy through holding, gazing into each other's eyes, and sensual touch is affirming at every life stage.

Congregations could take the lead in providing speakers to educate older couples and older singles about sexual alternatives. Even acknowledging the struggles of older sexuality (without Viagra jokes) can assist people to lower shame and explore emotional, spiritual, and sensual pleasures. I'll never forget the gleeful gratitude of an eighty-year-old woman in my office upon learning of a lubricant that restored her sexual pleasure. Offering workshops for people who are fifty-five and older using resources such as Dr. Ruth's *Sex after 50* as a study guide can help individuals and couples restore relational health and reduce sexual shame.[13] As I create a sexually healthy congregation in my mind, the grey-haired study group is having a lot of fun and finding joy and healing.

In addition to classes and programs, preaching is a powerful form of education. It takes place more often and more consistently than any other teaching format. Clergy who comfortably preach about sexuality show congregants ways to talk safely and respectfully, and invite conversations in other arenas of congregational life. Showing nonanxious leadership in the area of sexuality, grace will reduce shame.

Clergy need to familiarize themselves with Scripture stories about love and sex, many of which are left out of the standard lectionary. After preaching on the Song of Songs one Valentine's Day, I was greeted by a parishioner who said, "You gave me the chance to have my *whole body* in church today." After preaching on the King David saga of sexual harassment, incest, and generational patterns of abuse, a man approached me and said, "I have suffered silently as an incest survivor for far too many years. Where can I find help?" There are stories of abuse throughout the Scriptures that must be preached in order to liberate abuse survivors.

Shame-less preachers don't hold back in talking about love and sensuality. How brave of Joseph to take on the potential shame of accompanying Mary through her pregnancy! How wonderful of Sarah to pack everything up and head out on the promise of a new land with Abraham. How precious was Ruth's love for Naomi, love that led her to leave her own people to sojourn to a new land. All of these people went out by faith in God, but also by faith in each other. The Scriptures have playful, sensual elements within them too. When the goodness of sexuality is affirmed from the pulpit and when sexual issues are brought into open forums, the congregation is on its way to shame-lessness.

Can you now envision your sexually shame-less congregation? What steps could you take to bring this to fruition? Will you talk about sexual health in your faith community? Like any new skill, learning to talk about sex involves practice, a few mistakes, a little refinement, and repetition. What if you start talking about sex and feelings of shame come up? Don't panic, and don't stop. You now have the opportunity to learn from those feelings, tolerate them, and lower their intensity. There's no better way to become shame-less than to let shame arise without judgment, explore its origins, and move beyond it. Practicing the experience of shame, we learn to soothe ourselves when we feel it and repeatedly reclaim our birthright as beloved children of God.

CHAPTER 10

Grace Yourself
Practical Ways to Overcome Shame

When you engage in repetitive thinking, neuropathways in your brain become larger. This means that you can literally change your brain by negative thinking habits. The brain says, "I need more space to allow for all of this negativity," and in effect, creates it. As you may have guessed, the brain will also broaden neuropathways for positive thoughts and feelings as they pass through the synaptic system over time. When you expand the hopeful and positive neuronal structures in your brains, you diminish the flow of negativity, anxiety, and self-doubt. In Psalm 23, verse 3 is usually translated something like, God "leads me in paths of righteousness" (NAS) or "leads me in right paths" (NRSV). But a more literal translation is "leads me in right oxcart ruts." This wise psalmist asks us to notice the "ruts" we are in because those ruts make a difference! This chapter is designed to help you avoid shame-filled ruts. Having learned the origins of shame and ways to stop shaming others, we now turn our focus to habitual self-shaming and explore ways to put a stop to it. Additionally, we will look at ways to block incoming shame from faith communities and other people's criticisms.

Whether you learned shame from your family, your peers, a church or synagogue, a lousy boss, or a rejecting lover, at some point you have probably taken that shame to be your truth and made it your own. It may have once been the voice of your acidic father, your jealous sister, or your ex-wife, but amazingly it now sounds like your own voice and lives within your personality. The good news is that you have the opportunity to unlearn it and to practice a new way of being with yourself. You can get in the habit of gracing yourself. I know that "grace yourself" is an unusual expression. But because *shame* is a verb and *grace* is too, you might as well grace yourself more often and shame yourself a lot less. What if you said "Grace on me," instead of "Shame on me"? You can slander yourself, berate yourself, beat up on yourself—or you can accept yourself, love yourself, and grace yourself.

Shame easily becomes habitual, with negative outcomes. Saying things like "I'll never get this" is a prescription for failure. Words like "I can't" spoken repeatedly result in a fixed belief in your own incompetence. A student in one of my classes had a hard time picking a term paper topic. She spoke to me about it with intense self-criticism. "I've never been good at . . . ," "No matter how hard I try I usually fail," and "I just can't . . ." She has an enormous self-shaming lexicon that includes words like *always, never,* and *all the time.* To keep her from enlarging those negative neuropathways, I stopped her in the middle of a sentence. I asked her to please, for the rest of the term, stop using "I can't." "You might as well substitute 'I won't,'" I told her. "At least that way you'll know you are making a choice." She was taken aback. "How many times a day do you say 'I can't'?" I asked her. She blushed, "Nearly all day long." "Well, try dropping that from your vocabulary altogether and see what happens," I urged. By the end of the term she had found her topic and submitted an outstanding paper, and her self-appraisal was far more positive.

Many experiences culminate in shame, but we have the power to spot it and stop it ourselves. A woman whose father verbally abused her for forty years grew up hearing the language of shame and learned to use it on herself. Now she has to practice a new way of thinking and speaking. We have all stored data on the "hard drive" of our "operating systems." Here's how we change it. First, we have to find the data and then transfer it to a backup disk (in case for some reason we want to recall it again in the future), then we remove the backup disk, and last, go to "find and replace." Find the sentences that sting, and replace them with affirmations. "I'm a hopeless failure" becomes, "I may learn something from trying and failing that takes me toward success." I once heard a pastor say, "I can't ever please my congregation." She could instead offer herself this graceful affirmation: "Sometimes I will please them, and sometimes I won't, and that's okay with me."

Learning to change negative thoughts and accompanying emotions is the basis of the most widely used therapy in the past decade, cognitive-behavioral therapy (CBT), and a therapy gaining popularity called acceptance and commitment therapy (ACT). The techniques these therapies use are not complicated, and many of them can be incorporated into daily use and practice. Do try this at home! Catch those negative thoughts, observe them, and get them out of the operating system.

This may be hard work, depending on how long you have told yourself that you are a failure, ruined your chances, wasted your life, and can *never* change it. Shame can lead to depression, and unfortunately when depression becomes biological, the brain loses some of its ability to find happy ruts for stress mitigation. The biochemicals of happiness—serotonin, dopamine, and norepinephrine—can be depleted by repeated stress and trauma, leading to depression and more negative thinking. The size of the amygdala, which transmits signals to the brain from the spinal cord, has been found to be smaller in trauma survivors, which makes it more difficult to monitor and change thoughts in stressful situations. An anxiety sufferer in the throes of a panic attack also has a reduced ability to employ the prefrontal cortex, which normally provides stress relief. The film *What the Bleep Do We Know* shows actress Marlee Matlin playing a woman in the midst of depression.[1] When she attends a party, she feels overwhelmed with stress. The film shows animated images of the neuropeptides inside her brain. As her thinking becomes more and more negative, more damage is evident. A visual image of the brain in the throes of a terrible mood can inspire us to change thought patterns even when it is difficult to do so. Experts in spirituality and psychology talk about the essential need for meditation and mindfulness in creating positive pathways in the brain.

In some situations, old self-shaming habits engage the mind in excessive rumination. "What did I do wrong?" "Why can't I ever please my boss?" "How can I change my life when all my attempts fail?" If we have experienced trauma, we may have an even greater tendency to be vigilantly anxious. To find solace and peace, we need to slow such thoughts down before they race off with our happiness. The skill of self-quieting and self-soothing becomes the essential corrective skill. Daily prayer and silent meditation literally expand brain pathways for peace, content-ment, and awe.

Our interpretation of what's going on when we're feeling stress is what matters. The runner at the start of a race and the person terrified of presenting the keynote at a conference have the same physiological experience (palms sweating, heart racing, dry mouth, stomach pain). Interpreting those symptoms as stress or excitement makes all the difference at the finish line and in the lecture hall. A shame statement from the athlete, such as "I'm going to disappoint my coach and my team," will exacerbate the rush of adrenaline and produce unwanted physical symptoms. A comment such as "I can tell I'm really amped up and ready to go" will lead to a positive experience of the race and a better finish. The lecturer with positive self-talk will be less likely to stumble over words or to veer off the subject.

WHEN OTHER PEOPLE TRY TO SHAME YOU

The more you grace yourself, the less shame you are willing to take when it is tossed your way. In an earlier chapter I recalled a lecture I attended at a conference where, following his speech, a confident presenter took questions from the audience. The first man to shoot his hand up in the air and be recognized moved to the microphone in the center of the room. He mounted a caustic evaluation of the lecturer's position that stunned everyone. After a moment of total silence, the lecturer stepped closer to his own microphone, cleared his throat, and smiled slightly. He said, "I don't give you permission to shame me today. . . . Next question please." I came away admiring that guy for his refusal to accept shame, and I remember his retort more than the contents of his lecture. This approach is very high on my list of ways to resist shame. Name it for what it is, and refuse it.

I was sitting at my formidable desk in my church office one morning when a young woman arrived with an oversized King James Bible in her hand. I was still new to the congregation and she surprised me. You don't often see West Coast Methodists carrying their Bibles. She was one of our young moms and obviously on a mission. She placed her Bible on the edge of the desk where I could see evidence of its daily use and multiple bookmarks. When I offered her a seat, she sat forward on the edge of the chair.

"So, Rev-er-end," she said, making each syllable a word unto itself, "what *do* you believe about the virgin birth?" She continued without a pause for my answer. "It sounded on Sunday like you aren't so sure that Mary was a *virgin*." My thoughts took me down the road to women who are still pressured to retain their virginity. For some of them it is so sacred that it is protected, guarded, surgically sealed up, faked, and even inspected. Reining in my wandering mind I said, "Well, the story seems to follow the pattern of other biblical stories about divine offspring." Seeing her ready to pounce, I continued for another few sentences. "I heard your sermon," she blurted out, "but I can't come to your church unless you believe she was a *virgin*!" She was tearing up. I asked her to talk for a while longer, longer than I wish I had. While I appreciated her position, I did not appreciate the insinuation that I wasn't a *true* Christian if I wasn't clear on this point—and if not a true Christian, then clearly not fit for the vocation I was in. Her shameful tirade is still sitting on the hard drive of my memory. I wish I had been brave enough to stand up, shake her hand, usher her toward the door and say, "Thank you for coming, but I don't give you permission to shame me today."

The closer shame comes to home and family, the harder it is to take a stand against it. I frequently hear from young adults that they don't like calling home very often. Sometimes they are caught in a terrible loop system. They don't want to call mom or dad, because they are busy and simply enjoying their lives. Then when they do call home, they hear, "Well, it's about time you called." No one wants to start off a conversation being shamed, so they call home less and irk their parents more. Brave ones will find a way to express their feelings: "Let's start that conversation over again without the shame, okay?" A direct and polite comment, such as "Mom, please start the conversation on a positive note," can change the pattern.

Shame can quickly start a fight. "What did you do that for?" and "What's up with that?" are shame-based challenges. A sentence that starts with "Do you think you can . . . ?" with the tone of voice that implies you probably can't, will escalate a fight. "What were you thinking?" belongs on the list of questions to avoid at all cost. To stop shame, we all have to be careful not to let it go beyond one comment or one sentence. If you let someone throw shame your way, it can easily escalate to the point that you lash back with blame. You are the only one who can take back your power when other people shame you. You have to name the behavior and refuse to engage in it.

When shame sticks in your head like an obnoxious tune, here's something else to try. Take a journal and open it to a place with blank pages on either side. On the left side, write down the self statements that are floating around in your head. On the right side, use the content of the statement but follow it with a positive affirmation. For example, you might write "I feel too tired to turn out a good sermon this week" on the left side. On the right side, you would write the sentence again, and follow it with "and when I rest I'll soon be more creative." Avoid words like *try* and *if* and *can't*. Use words like *will* and *when* and *can*. Say you put this sentence on the left side: "I can't lead the Bible study group, because I'm just not spiritual enough." Then write a more graceful comment on the right side. It might be, "I bet that other people in my group sometimes feel spiritually dry, and we can begin by talking about that." Doing this process frequently will help you to replace self-shaming language with self-loving language. Then, in times of stress, you will have more access to positive thoughts.

Another strategy to deflect shame involves taking ownership of your faults. If the woman who wanted my allegiance to Mary's literal virginity had been at all open to dialogue, I might have said, "You've learned something about me. I have questions about some things in the Bible, and I feel okay with that." Hearing me confess my truth, she might lower her defenses. If she were healthy enough to be in dialogue with me, the anger would have been diffused.

When new couples start their lives together, they often learn things that surprise them. "I didn't know that about you!" is a cry for stability in the relationship. "You can't be like that!" is the underlying shame message. "I thought you knew me" is a cry to be seen and understood. I remember the day that I mentioned to my husband of just about one year that he was contradicting himself. I was angry. But he smiled and said, "I *am* a bundle of contradictions" and hugged me. He lowered all of my fears that our differences would lead to conflicts and painful dissatisfaction. We lower shame and stop the shame-blame game when we respond to the evaluations of others gracefully.

HUMOR DEFLECTING SHAME

Humor can also deflect shame, but it must be clearly distinguished from sarcasm. Sarcasm is often hostility disguised in humor and, in fact, can be very shaming. Sarcasm against yourself can also be off-putting to others. I had a friend for a short while who repeatedly used "jokes" against herself. She would laugh when no one around her laughed. It was a nervous habit, and others saw her self-deprecating humor as a measure of her low self-esteem. We were uncomfortable around her. What she considered humor was a mask over her insecurity.

Genuine humor arises from moments in which we enjoy our human foibles. One day while walking through the lobby of our local hospital after an intense visit in the emergency room, I turned my head to look at the clock on the wall and walked straight into a concrete pillar. No warning, just smack and rebound. If it had been a cartoon, there would have been birds and stars circling over my head. I watched the spellbound people in the lobby trying so hard not to laugh that their eyes were watering up. So I sat down on one of the couches to recoup and started laughing. Before long the room was full of laughter and relief.

People tell me that I am a compelling worship leader and public speaker due to my ease in the leadership role and my sense of humor. It wasn't always like that for me. Early on in my ministry I was trying so hard to be good, right, caring, and competent that I was a bundle of anxiety. I preached from a written sermon, because I was afraid of saying something wrong, and even then felt the sting of every critical comment. I felt ashamed when they compared me to their beloved former pastor, and when I looked out across some empty seats at worship, I felt I was falling short by not drawing more people in. Not yet understanding how to be whole, I was striving to be perfect. It's hard to be lighthearted in an environment where shame is evident and debilitating. As I became shame-less and led congregations to be shame-less, too, we all became more playful, relaxed, and affirming.

A mentor for me in pastoral ministry a long time ago told me to be sure that people laugh at some point in every sermon. It was excellent advice. The healing benefits of laughing are well espoused. I used to be sure to tell a joke in every sermon, but as I grew less and less afraid of the evaluations of my congregation, humor became more natural. Sometimes humor was the best way to handle an unexpected embarrassment. During one of my first sermons in a new parish, I slipped the microphone cord over my head and it got caught in my hoop earring. All previous pastors had been men (in a decade before men wore earrings), and they didn't know that their sound system came with a hoop-earring hazard. After what seemed like many minutes of trying to free myself, I simply had to laugh, and so did they—and soon a lay leader came forward and rescued me. The giggles reduced the embarrassment and kept us out of shame. In moments where we can be human together, joy and humor flow easily. The laughter connects us to one another.

When I preach these days, I am often a guest in an unfamiliar pulpit. I am bound to make several mistakes as I lead everyone through the order of worship. I could be stern and upset with myself, or I can simply smile and admit that (oops!) I skipped the doxology. What I find is that people seem to genuinely relax when they are led by someone who is shame-less. We simply back up and sing the doxology out of order. The change may catch them by surprise, but it also allows the worship experience to feel fresh and lively. Do-overs in church? Yes. They are absolutely necessary in creating a shame-less congregation.

Leaders who can laugh at their mistakes create space for humor. Under the burden of shame, the world is overly serious. Leaders who lighten up a bit lower the tension people feel about having to be at their best or appearing to be *good* believers when they are in the congregation. At the start of a meeting you are leading, ask the participants to tell funny stories about their lives, and begin with their humanity rather than with their godliness. Ask questions like, "What was your most embarrassing moment in public?" or "Describe a funny thing that happened this week." The work of the Holy Spirit isn't limited to times of illness, conflict, transition, or death. The Holy Spirit provides joyfulness and playfulness in congregations in order to dispel shame.

Clergy who are about to be assigned or called to a new congregation can benefit from writing down questions to ask at their interview. To assess for persistent shame they need to ask about secrets that have been kept in the congregation. And then I suggest that they ask the question, "When and how do you play together?" If the answers are vague or "We don't," then they have likely come across a depressed and shame-based congregation. Shame-less congregational leaders intentionally foster playfulness, recreation, and humor.

SHUCK OFF THE SECRETS

Playfulness is limited in systems where secrets are kept. Everyone is too busy monitoring the content of their conversations and controlling behaviors, so secrets are not revealed. Secrets keep feelings of shame from arising, but they also prevent the liberating truths that lead to grace. Claudia Black, psychologist and author, writes:

> Recovery is a life free from shame. It is recognizing that you are not your secret; you are not your family secrets. You are a person with a myriad of experiences, some of them very painful. But, the pain of exposing the secret, very, very rarely compares to the pain of keeping the secret."[2]

For many of us whose families kept secrets when we were kids, the experience of talking about them will always include anxiety. But the shame of talking about them fades away with practice. And as the shame lifts, relief follows.

When congregations carry secrets, the mood of the congregation becomes overly serious. Sometimes visitors detect this as depression and say, "There's just so little life there." Congregations can become stuck in devastating oxcart ruts. At the time of a crisis, behaviors change. When that crisis involves a secret, the organizational system adapts to protect the secret keeper and the reputation of the congregation. When the painful situation is resolved, the behaviors need to be consciously changed or the congregation will keep acting *as if* it still has the problem.

The results of shame-laden secrets can continue for years. Power struggles, leadership conflicts, and limited growth are the outcomes of a congregation overdosed on shame. With careful disclosure leaders eliminate those old ruts and take up new paths of righteousness. They learn to say as much as possible about the past and to safely open up old wounds without reinjuring victims. To carefully explore the complex process of disclosure you may want to read *Healthy Disclosure*, an earlier work I have written with Kibbie Ruth, an abuse-prevention specialist and director of Kyros Ministry.[3] Speaking the truth in love can release the entire system from secrets and shame.

When Shame Arises from Trauma or Death

In 2011 when across the United States storms flooded synagogues and churches, schools, businesses, and family homes, and tornados ripped through communities, congregations joined together to provide comfort, address basic needs, and offer trauma support. Clergy and congregational leaders proved themselves to be remarkably resilient in contributing assistance and rebuilding worship centers and their neighborhoods. The trauma of natural disasters brings out the best in many people, and the devastation of homes and the loss of loved ones can be overcome with gestures of help and kindness.

Any form of trauma and any death can be mingled with shame. While no one could be held directly responsible for a tornado, most survivors nevertheless suffer from guilt and shame—guilt that they survived and shame people refer to as "shoulda, woulda, coulda." A mother who dropped her daughter off to play at a house where she was killed by the storm will forever feel that she *should have* known the storm was coming, *could have* gone after her daughter while the storm barreled down on the town, and will forever wish that she *would have* made a different decision that morning. When grief becomes wedded with shame, feelings of remorse are very hard to overcome.

Parents who lose children are particularly vulnerable to shame, because it is the job of parents to protect their children. This is true for parents whose children are sexually or physically abused by strangers, neighbors, so-called friends, or family members with whom they left their children for care. Anguished parents who survive their children, whose children are harmed, or whose children become ill commonly express regrets with phrases such as

"I should have known," "Why didn't I see it coming?" or "I could have stopped it."

I once had a pastoral visit with an eighty-year-old mother of three children. Lenore had lost her second child when he was eight. He had run into the street after a ball and had been killed by a passing car. The tears that arose during the story were almost as fresh as they were on the day of the funeral. She described years of replaying that day in her mind and how hard it was to start back into life after it happened. "I will never forgive myself," she said, "never." Why would she keep holding herself responsible? "Because it was my job to see that he was safe, and I failed at my job." "And what will happen when you meet Saint Peter at the pearly gates?" I asked, "Will you be in trouble for this?" "I doubt it," she laughed. "It'll just be good to see my boy again." For more than fifty years she had been stuck in shame, and the only relief she could envision was a life with Jesus and her son in heaven. Sadly, for the whole family, her shame negatively affected her life with her husband and her other children. Her older children lost the mother they once had on the day their brother died. Her joy, her self-acceptance, her pleasure in parenting all shifted under the weight of this shame. To become shame-less, she would have to accept herself, be more generous with herself, and accept God's grace over and over again when voices of guilt (I made a mistake) and shame (I am a mistake) arose in the aftermath of the trauma. While she was holding hope in a shame-less future in heaven with her son, I wish she had graced herself in the intervening years.

Losing a loved one is so painful that it's a common psychological strategy to go looking for someone to blame. A widow at a support group recounted the last days of her life with her husband. She kept repeating to the group that she had not done enough for him "at the end, when he needed me most." They challenged her on this idea with various questions and found no reason to incriminate her. Yet, she needed to berate herself for being a "bad" wife. She was gracious toward him, even though he had neglected his own health for many years. But she had a hard time not blaming and shaming herself. The closer a loved one is to the person who dies, the more grief and shame comingle. The grief is natural and enduring. The shame doesn't need to be.

Many people think every death has to be someone's fault. In cases of suicide the blame and shame becomes even more intense. When children lose a parent, they often engage in what's called magical thinking and find reasons to blame themselves for the death. When a suicide takes place in a family, shame about the death may be extremely high. Many Christians believe that suicide is an act of sin that results in the loved one going to hell. This belief raises painful feelings of shame for the family whose loved one, they think, was disobedient to God's will. They may also grieve the loss of being united with their loved one in heaven. When suicide takes place, everyone experiences varying levels of shame for not noticing signs of the loved one's intentions ahead of time. Individual and group counseling, bereavement support groups at congregations, and pastoral care with the intent of lowering shame and providing grace can all help loved ones become shame-less.

ON YOUR WAY TO SHAME-LESSNESS

Whenever "shouda, woulda, coulda" thinking comes along in life, set it aside. Replace that inner voice before it makes ruts in your brain. Who gets to decide what you *shoulda* done? Does some ancient dictate, the voice of your stern parent, or your inner critic become the judge and jury? Try saying, "I did the best I could with what I knew at the time." Sure, with all of the information you have now, you can see that you *woulda* done it differently, but back then you didn't know the storm was coming, your friend was depressed, your brother would drive home drunk, your babysitter would fondle your child. You didn't know. You can be more alert now, you can warn people now, you can be vigilant in protecting your loved ones, and more important, you can tell them every day that you love them now. *Now* you can do that. Shaming yourself for the past is exhausting. Whatever you still hold yourself hostage for is burdening you down and limiting your joy. You *coulda* taken a different path, but all of us have roads we didn't go down for better and for worse. You can become shame-less. Mistakes don't add up to making you a bad person. They just make you a human person. Yes, it can be very painful to be human, but it can also be very lovely.

You started becoming shame-less when you picked up this book and began reading it. You are obviously ready to clear out some old shame that has been influencing your self-confidence, your moods, or your relationships. With a little faith and courage, you can now conquer old habits like perfectionism, comparisons, blame-shame, and sexual shame. Your relationships are already becoming healthier as you accept your differences, affirm your own needs, and accept your mistakes with a lightness of spirit (and only a modicum of remorse). Perhaps you are crawling on your knees less and dancing more.

It's time to affirm your sexual thoughts and desires, and be sure that your behaviors are in line with your promises and your values. Healthy sexuality includes the ability to ask for what you want, take responsibility for your own orgasm, explore, accept your body rather than criticize it, and find safe partners or provide yourself with tender self-pleasuring touches. To keep shame at bay, use protection from pregnancy and sexually transmitted diseases, avoid coercing or being coerced, and handle powerful physiologic responses with self-affirming statements. Increase self-trust and then you can give up power, share power, and exchange power. Avoid comparison shame in the bedroom ("My last partner was so much better at . . . !"). Avoid perfection shame during sexual intimacy too ("Who'd want this sagging body?"). And avoid the shame-blame game ("I could have had a really great orgasm if only you hadn't stopped to scratch your head in the middle of things!"). Affirm the goodness of your body and its miraculous capacity to uplift you, to bond you to your partner, to fill you with holiness and awe.

Eradicating shame may take a few weeks, months, years, or a lifetime. This book is not written so that you can be free of *all* shame. It is written so that you become shame-less by acknowledging old patterns and consciously changing them.

Several years after I blessedly found my way to a shame-less life, I gathered with clergy colleagues who had known me across nearly twenty-five years of ministry. The feedback my closest friends gave me was puzzling at first. They kept saying that despite my literal years of growing older, I was looking younger, happier, and more vibrant. They could see that the weight of shame had been lifted from my shoulders. I knew that on the inside I had wrestled with and eradicated a lot of shame, but until I received their feedback, I had no idea that it was so evident on the outside. This is the transformation I wish for you as well.

Liberation from shame inspired me to write this book. I firmly believe that you will be better off with less shame. Speaking truth, emerging from dark places, honoring your story, moving beyond your secrets or the secrets in your family, you will enjoy the freedom of a shame-less life. And if the old "I'll never be good enough," or "if I'm hurting it must be my fault," comes back into your thoughts, please change them before they make wider ruts. Jesus clearly has a more compassionate way for you. In John's Gospel (John 10:10; 15:11) Jesus promises an abundant life, and proclaims "I have said these things to you so that my joy may be in you, and that your joy may be complete." I can think of no more fitting proclamation of grace!

Appendix A

My Sexual Ethic

An ethic is a set of rules and principles for conduct. Unlike a moral, which applies words like *right* and *wrong* to all similar circumstances, an ethic allows for sets of principles that are applied to different situations. A sexual ethic includes values such as trust, honesty, and respect. Before you begin this exercise, make a list of values you hold as you think about healthy relationships. Then, define your own beliefs about sexuality using this writing exercise.

1. For me, sexual intimacy is . . .
2. For me, sexual intimacy is right only when . . .
3. I will share my nakedness when . . .
4. What I cherish about my body and my sexuality is . . .
5. Cultural, family, and religious teachings that inform my understanding of sexuality are . . .
6. I consider the following sexual thoughts, desires, or behaviors as sin or off-limits:
7. I have a hunch that my faith community or significant others probably think that my sexual desires or behaviors are . . .
8. I have the following obligations to others regarding my sexual behavior:
9. I have the following obligations to others regarding potentially harmful sexual behavior:
10. I believe that healthy sexuality includes . . .

Reprinted by permission of the Alban Institute from Karen A. McClintock, *Shame-Less Lives, Grace-Full Congregations*, copyright © 2011 by the Alban Institute, Inc.

APPENDIX B

When Sex Moves Out of Bounds

The list below illustrates the complexity of sexuality and relationships. Sexual behaviors have the power to enhance our love for one another and to bring us closer to God. They have the physical benefits of improving mood, increasing immune functioning, and lowering risk of heart attack and stroke. They affect our relationships at home, in the workplace, and in faith communities.

Before you study the list, draw a box on a piece of paper and put inside the box all of the sexual behaviors you think are okay, sacred, or uplifting. Then put things on the edges that you aren't so sure about. Finally, put things you definitely think are harmful, immoral, or unethical outside that box. You've begun to define behaviors that you consider out of bounds. I expect that you will disagree with some of the things on my list, which is fine. Feel free to make your own list and to share this list with others.

Psychological Dangers

- Using psychological manipulation to compel someone to engage in or witness sexual behavior
- Using sexual stimulation as a distraction from feelings or fears
- Repeatedly using sexual fantasy, visual stimulation, or multiple partners to get high in order to avoid painful issues
- Having sex in a state of disconnection from yourself, your partner, or God

- Denying your own sexual desires, attractions, and arousal, which could lead to acting out on those feelings without forethought
- Objectifying a human being through the use of pornography or social media

Physical Dangers

- Harming your body or someone else's body
- Infecting someone with a sexually transmitted disease or risking infection yourself
- Having sex while intoxicated or using drugs
- Giving up on sensuous touch and sexual intimacy when it becomes embarrassing or changes across the lifespan

Relational Dangers

- Damaging relationships by shaming others for their sexual desires, attractions, or behavior
- Using age, gender, ethnicity, status, or spiritual authority to manipulate or gain power over others to create a sexual fantasy or engage in sexual activity
- Breaking an agreement of fidelity or monogamy
- Using sex or withholding sex as a weapon in a power struggle
- Knowing that someone is engaging in self-harming sexual behavior and keeping silent

Congregation or Workplace Dangers

- Seeing or having knowledge of a boundary crossing and not reporting it
- Allowing a person in a professional role (or anyone else) to use his or her age, gender, ethnicity, status, or spiritual authority to make demeaning sexual comments or to

harass another through innuendo, humor, leering, touching, or gestures
- Participating in harassing behavior and minimizing, denying, or ignoring it

Notes

Introduction

1. Maldwyn L. Edwards, *John Wesley,* digital edition, ed. Clyde C. Price Jr. (Lake Junaluska, NC: World Methodist Council Association of Methodist Historical Societies, July 1994–5).

Chapter 1: Where Shame Begins

1. Gershen Kaufman, *The Psychology of Shame,* 2nd ed. (New York: Springer, 1996), 4.

Chapter 2: Yours, Mine, and Ours

1. Thomas Aquinas, *Basic Writings of Saint Thomas Aquinas,* vol. 2, ed. Anton C. Pegis (Indianapolis: Hackett, 1997), 637.
2. Abigail Goldman, "One Nation, Seven Sins," *Las Vegas Sun,* March 26, 2009, http://www.lasvegassun.com/news/2009/mar/26/one-nation-seven-sins/.
3. Edwin H. Friedman, *Generation to Generation: Family Process in Church and Synagogue* (New York: Guilford, 1985), 26.

Chapter 3: We're All Different

1. Ruth Benedict, *The Chrysanthemum and the Sword* (Boston: Houghton Mifflin, 1946).
2. Margaret Mead, *Culture and Commitment* (1928; repr. Garden City, NY: Anchor, 1978).
3. Gerhart Piers and Milton B. Singer, *Shame and Guilt: A Psychoanalytical and a Cultural Study* (1953; repr. New York: Norton, 1971).

4. Harald G. Wallbott and Klaus Scherer, "Cultural Determinants in Experiencing Shame and Guilt," in *Self-conscious Emotions: The Psychology of Shame, Guilt, Embarrassment, and Pride,* eds. June Price Tangney and Kurt W. Fischer (New York: Guilford Press, 1995), 465–87.

5. David Matsumoto and Linda Juang, *Culture and Psychology,* 3rd ed. (Belmont, CA: Thomson Wadsworth, 2004), 243–47.

6. Karen A. McClintock, *Sexual Shame: An Urgent Call to Healing* (Minneapolis: Augsburg Fortress, 2001), 123–24.

7. K. C. Hanson, *How Honorable! How Shameful! A Cultural Analysis of Matthew's Makarisms and Reproaches* (Eugene, OR: Wipf and Stock, 2011), 44.

Chapter 4: The Shame-Blame Game

1. Robert Funk, *Honest to Jesus* (New York: HarperCollins, 1996), 155.

2. Robert H. Albers, *Shame: A Faith Perspective* (New York: Haworth Pastoral Press, 1995), 78.

3. The Gottman Relationship Institute website, www.gottman.com.

Chapter 5: Comparison Shame

1. The Internet Movie Database, "Memorable Quotes for *Annie Hall* (1977)," http://www.imdb.com/title/tt0075686/quotes.

2. Research into the workings of the brain has found that how we think about the past matters. Clinical neuroscientist Daniel G. Amen says, "Through SPECT imaging, I have found that when people think about happy memories from the past, it enhances brain function. Instead of erasing your past completely make sure the version of it that runs through your head has a positive spin." Amen, *Change Your Brain, Change Your Body* (New York: Three Rivers Press, 2010) 232.

3. Russ Harris, *ACT Made Simple* (Oakland, CA: New Harbinger, 2009), 156–57.

Chapter 6: Perfection Shame

1. Harold S. Kushner, *How Good Do We Have to Be? A New Understanding of Guilt and Forgiveness* (New York: Little, Brown, 1996), 38–39.
2. Sigmund Freud, *The Ego and the Id* (1923; repr. London: Hogarth Press, 1961), 19, 1–66.
3. Flora Slosson Wuellner, *Release for Trapped Christians* (Nashville: Abingdon Press, 1974), 15–16.
4. Ibid., 16.
5. John M. Berecz and Herbert W. Helm Jr., "Shame: the Underside of Christianity," *Journal of Psychology and Christianity* 17, no. 1 (1998): 8.
6. Ibid.
7. Ibid., 8–9.
8. Ibid., 9.
9. Barbara Brown Taylor, *Leaving Church: A Memoir of Faith* (New York: Harper Collins, 2006), 218–19.
10. Wuellner, *Release for Trapped Christians*, 18.
11. Ibid., 17–18.
12. *Diagnostic and Statistical Manual of Mental Disorders (DSM-IV)*, 4th ed. (Washington, DC: American Psychiatric Association, 1994), 658.
13. Ibid., 661.

Chapter 7: Chronic Illness Shame

1. Martin Seligman as cited in David H. Barlow and V. Mark Durand, *Abnormal Psychology: An Integrative Approach, 5th ed.* (Belmont, CA: Wadsworth Cengage Learning, 2009), 54–55.
2. Brene Brown, *"The Power of Vulnerability,"* TED lecture, June 2010, www.Ted.com/talks/brene_brown_on_vulnerability.html.
3. For more information and a group in your area, see the National Alliance for the Mentally Ill website, www.nami.org.
4. B. Egolf, J. Lasker, S. Wolf, and L. Potvin, "The Roseto Effect: A 50-Year Comparison of Mortality Rates," *American Journal of Public Health* 82, no. 8 (1992): 1089–92.

Chapter 8: Naked and Ashamed

1. Diane Arbus, "Mae West: Emotion in Motion," *Show Magazine*, January 1965, 42.

2. A fuller treatment of this subject is available in my book *Sexual Shame: An Urgent Call to Healing* (Minneapolis: Fortress Press, 2001).

3. The editor of this book found sources that claim the Smythers document is from *The Madison Institute Newsletter*, Fall Issue, 1894 and another that it's from Spiritual Guidance Press, New York and reprinted in the newsletter. The United Methodist Church denominational archivist told us that neither Reverend Smythers nor the Arcadian Methodist Church of the Eastern Regional Conference existed. More information on this controversial document can be found at www.themediadesk.com/newfiles2/youngbride.htm.

4. Janell L. Carroll, *Sexuality Now: Embracing Diversity*, 3rd ed. (Belmont, CA: Wadsworth, 2010), xxxvi.

5. Smythers. See note 3.

6. James Moore, "The Lies of Texas Are Upon You," *The Huffington Post*, September 4, 2009, http://www.huffingtonpost.com/jim-moore/the-lies-of-texas-are-upo_b_277749.html.

7. *Kinsey*, directed by Bill Condon (Beverly Hills, CA: Twentieth Century Fox Home Entertainment, 2005).

8. Alfred C. Kinsey, *Sexual Behavior in the Human Male* (1948; repr. Bloomington, IN: Indiana University Press, 1975).

9. Kate M. Ott, "Sex and the Seminary: Preparing Ministers for Sexual Health and Justice" (New York: Religious Institute on Sexual Morality, Justice, and Healing, 2009), *http.religiousinstitute.org/research-report/sex-and-the-seminary-preparing-ministers-for-sexual-health-and-justice*.

10. Alfred C. Kinsey, letter to unknown correspondent, "Primary Sources: Letters to Kinsey," *Kinsey: American Experience*, PBS Online, www.pbs.org/wgbh/amex/kinsey/filmmore/ps_letters.html.

11. Ibid.

12. Betty Dodson, *Sex for One: The Joy of Selfloving* (New York: Three Rivers Press, 1996).

13. Judy Norsigian, *Our Bodies, Ourselves* (New York: Touchstone Press, 1984).

14. Alex Comfort, *The New Joy of Sex* (New York: Crown Publishers, 1991).

15. Inga Muscio, *Cunt: A Declaration of Independence* (New York: Seal Press, 2002).

16. "Toronto 'Slut Walk' Takes to City Streets," CBCNews Canada, April 3, 2011, http://cbc.ca/news/canada/toronto/story/2011/04/03/slut-walk-toronto.html.

Chapter 9: Sexual Shame in Congregations

1. Ellen Bass and Laura Davis, *The Courage to Heal* (New York: HarperCollins, 1994).

2. A list of curriculum options can be found in Debra W. Haffner, *A Time to Build: Creating Sexually Healthy Faith Communities* (Westport, CT: Religious Institute on Sexual Morality, Justice, and Healing, 2002), 24–25.

3. Chiara Sabina, Janis Wolak, and David Finkelhor, "The Nature and Dynamics of Internet Pornography Exposure for Youth," *CyberPsychology & Behavior* 11, no. 6 (December 2008): 691–93.

4. The Henry J. Kaiser Foundation, "Report of U.S. Teen Sexual Activity," January 2005, www.kff.org.

5. Jannell L. Caroll, *Sexuality Now: Embracing Diversity* (Belmont, CA: Wadsworth/Cengage, 2007), 206.

6. Gretel C. Kovach, "Pastor's Advice for Better Marriage: More Sex," *New York Times*, November 23, 2008.

7. J. J. Thomas, "Virginity Pledgers Are Just as Likely as Matched Nonpledgers to Report Premarital Intercourse," *Perspectives on Sexual and Reproductive Health* 41, no. 1 (March 2009): 63.

8. Gail Murphy-Geiss, *Review of Religious Research* 48, no. 3 (2007): 260–72.

9. Karen McClintock, "Silence: A Dangerous Bargain," in the United Methodist Commission on the Status and Role of Women, *The Flyer* 41, no. 11 (November 2010): 4. Available

online at www.gcsrw.org/InTheLoop/TheFlyer.aspx, or at the Sexual Ethics website, umsexualethics.org/ConferenceLeaders/ BishopsCabinetsandChancellors/Handbook.aspx.

10. John Jay College Research Team, *The Causes and Context of Sexual Abuse of Minors by Catholic Priests in the United States, 1950–2010* (Washington, DC: United States Conference of Catholic Bishops, 2011).

11. Jim FitzGerald, quoted in "John Jay Report Discredits Accusations that Gay Priests Are to Blame: Incidence of Abuse No Greater Among Gay Clergy," *Equally Blessed,* www.equally-blessed.org/node/13.

12. Debra W. Haffner, *A Time to Build: Creating Sexually Healthy Faith Communities* (Westport, CT: Religious Institute on Sexual Morality, Justice, and Healing, 2002), 14. See also the Religious Institute website at www.religiousinstitute.org.

13. Ruth Westheimer, *Sex after 50* (Fresno, CA: Quill Driver Books, 2005).

Chapter Ten: Grace Yourself: Practical Ways to Overcome Shame

1. William Arntz, producer, *What the Bleep Do We Know?* (Los Angeles: Roadside Attractions, 2004).

2. Claudia Black, *Changing Course: Healing from Loss, Abandonment, and Fear* (Bainbridge Island, WA: MAC Publishing, 2006), 131.

3. Kibbie Ruth and Karen McClintock, *Healthy Disclosure: Solving Communication Quandaries in Congregations* (Herndon, VA: Alban Institute, 2008).